Praise for Find Your Happy

"I love this! Shannon's perspective is sunny and bright and will light your day with heart and bliss! *Find Your Happy* is a fabulous gift for anyone you know, anytime!"
—**Kristine Carlson**, New York Times Best-selling author of *Don't Sweat the Small Stuff for Women* and *Moms*

"Shannon Kaiser is an incredible woman on a mission to help people find peace, happiness and fulfillment in their lives. Her desire to serve others shines through all of her work."
—**Gabrielle Bernstein**, Best-selling author of *Spirit Junkie* and *May Cause Miracles*

"Shannon Kaiser not only believes in the message of happiness, she lives it and breathes it. Every time I talk to Shannon, happiness finds a way in. Pick up this book and breathe in some happiness for yourself!"
—**Christine Arylo**, self-love author of *Madly in Love with ME, the Daring Adventure to Becoming Your Own Best Friend*

"I've worked in the wellness industry for decades, and I've read a lot of great inspirational books. Through her candid sharing of personal experiences and depth of understanding, Shannon is able to bring forth universal wisdom and truths in a fresh, lively voice that speaks directly to me. *Find Your Happy* stands out for its simple, easy-to-implement principles and honest perspective. Shannon's book is a therapeutic adventure for your soul, and it will transform the way you see yourself and the world. Get ready to fall in love with your entire life!"
—**Robyn Griggs Lawrence**, author of *The Wabi-Sabi House*

"There are a lot of people dishing out feel good meditations and words of wisdom. But Shannon Kaiser is a true sparkling star, who authentically shares her message of hope and happiness in this profound intimate guide. By picking up this book you are not only choosing to see life in a new perspective you are saying yes to yourself, you are worth it, and your dreams will be realized."
—**Shanon Hoffman**, Publisher of *Healing Lifestyles & Spas*

FIND YOUR HAPPY

*An Inspirational Guide to
Loving Life to Its Fullest*

Shannon Kaiser

BALBOA
PRESS

A DIVISION OF HAY HOUSE

ISBN: 978-1-4525-5541-6(sc)
ISBN: 978-1-4525-5542-3(e)
ISBN: 978-1-4525-5543-0(bh)

Library of Congress Control Number: 2012914018

Balboa Press books may be ordered through booksellers or by contacting:

Balboa Press
A Division of Hay House
1663 Liberty Drive
Bloomington, IN 47403
www.balboapress.com
1-(877) 407-4847

Because of the dynamic nature of the Internet, any web addresses or links contained in this book may have changed since publication and may no longer be valid. The views expressed in this work are solely those of the author and do not necessarily reflect the views of the publisher, and the publisher hereby disclaims any responsibility for them.

Cover Design by Shannon Kaiser

The author of this book does not dispense medical advice or prescribe the use of any technique as a form of treatment for physical, emotional, or medical problems without the advice of a physician, either directly or indirectly. The intent of the author is only to offer information of a general nature to help you in your quest for emotional and spiritual well-being. In the event you use any of the information in this book for yourself, which is your constitutional right, the author and the publisher assume no responsibility for your actions.

Any people depicted in stock imagery provided by Thinkstock are models, and such images are being used for illustrative purposes only. Certain stock imagery © Thinkstock.

Printed in the United States of America

Balboa Press rev. date:10/24/2012

For my beautiful Mother.

You are the most amazing Mom and friend in the world.

I win.

Table of Contents

Preface

It's Not Life That Matters;
It's the Courage That We Bring to It

I took a sip of my morning tea hoping that the new day would be better than any day before. I had somehow tripped over the cracks of life and couldn't seem to pull myself back up. I had woken up feeling eager to start a new day, but like every other day of my life, within the first few hours, things had gotten off track.

I was stuck in a downward vortex of fear, anxiety, and self-ridicule. I remember reading my Yogi tea bag message, "It's not life that matters; it's the courage that we bring to it." I held back my tears because my courage was feeling impossibly deflated. I was sick of trying so hard just to live my own life.

How much courage do we really need to live our life? I realized that I had felt like a fraud my entire life. I was renting someone else's story, trying to pretend that it was mine. My only consistency was in not being true and honoring myself. It is exhausting to be someone you're not supposed to be.

Society conditioned me to believe that if you want something, you have to work hard to get it. I worked really hard, accepting the fact that life was supposed to be an uphill struggle. All of my relationships were superficial. I was in a job that I hated. I felt like a dried-up, bitter woman who married her spouse for the wrong reasons — money, acceptance, and approval — only to be faced with the sinking sensation of being alone and feeling desperation in a loveless partnership. My job in corporate provided me with nothing but a deep dark depression and an avoidance of confronting who I really was. I forced a smile as I masked the inward sinking reality that I felt alone, unworthy, and afraid to acknowledge that fear was my real drug of choice. Addicted to the avoidance of pain and the stories I would tell myself, I stayed stuck for the majority of my life.

Everyone I knew wanted to talk about the latest fashion buzz, who won *American Idol,* or which celebrity died of yet another overdose. I pretended to be interested, but the truth was I wasn't any different from the celebrities who chose to run from their pain. The ability to escape life was far too easy. Whatever the drug of choice was, I found myself starting to see there could be a better way. I was more curious about the pull on my heart. It kept prickling and nagging as if to say, "There is more than this, honey."

For over a decade I lived this delusional nightmare of codependency and the search for security without success. All my romantic relationships were carefully chosen to escape the painful reality of anxiety. I'd pick partners who were addicted to numbing their pain, too. We'd escape life by doing drugs together and drinking over the fear. When I finally got up enough courage to recognize that a relationship was unhealthy, I would end it, only to find myself back in the arms of another addiction; overeating, over exercising, overworking, overspending, more men, and more drugs. I stayed in a constant state of denial consumed by my fear-based mind.

I was always waiting for the next thing to happen, the next promotion, the next boyfriend, the next anything to drag me out of my depression. It never occurred to me that "pushing" was the problem. My inner drive and constant forcing things to happen was really just a cry for help, an outburst, and a need for love.

I believed the root of my depression was my job in advertising. At the time, I didn't realize my source of depression was not my career. I've since learned that depression is not an emotion or feeling, it is an avoidance of feeling our feelings. I was living one big, carefully-crafted lie created to avoid feeling my real truth. Afraid to look at the shadows and nasty cracks in my own personality, it was much easier to get drugs, buy a $100 T-shirt that I didn't really want, or gulp down a half-gallon of cookie dough ice cream as I cried hysterically between bites. It was much less painful (so I thought) to exercise for four hours or throw up my 3,000 calorie burrito as if it never happened only to feel more alone and even more empty inside. It was easier to run away and have a temporary moment of relief than to possibly think about what would happen if I addressed the pain. What would happen if I felt the feelings and moved through the depression? I couldn't ask myself what was on the other side of that pain, because the pain itself felt so drastic; I'd rather sit in a burning fire than face those demons.

I thought it was normal for people to cry themselves to sleep every night. In fact my cry fests crept into the workplace. It was a daily routine to cry in the bathroom at work. The higher I climbed on the corporate ladder, the more alone, empty, and scared I felt. I was living a life that wasn't made for me. I didn't relate to anyone in the advertising field, and I didn't care about selling people things that they didn't need. It all felt so false and misdirected.

One night, regretting the fact that I had just forced my dinner into the toilet and mad at my friend for refusing to give me more painkillers, I found myself choking on my tears, crying on the cold bathroom floor. I had hit my rock bottom.

I looked around and didn't recognize any of my reality. The giant timber beam loft in downtown Chicago, the title of Senior Art Director at one of the world's top advertising agencies, the giant paychecks — none of it felt real. None of it was what I really wanted. I had carefully crafted every aspect of this life, thinking that it would all make me happy, but with each new promotion and each new "thing," I came crashing harder to the ground. I had just worked three 14-hour days in a row. The exhaustion, combined with lack of self-care had taken its toll on me.

I was suffocating in the madness because I was trying so hard to be someone I wasn't. I was pretending to fit into a mold that was so clearly opposite of me. I bowed my head in exhaustion and prayed. I yelled and screamed into the thin air. I pleaded with God, asking Him for help. Within an instant the air stripped down and calm filled the room. The tears immediately dried. I felt something very new. I felt peace come over me. A calm presence filled the space between my neurotic self and the real me. I heard my inner voice gently say, "Follow your heart."

I stood up, pulled the cap off my overpriced red lipstick and made a master list of what I wanted. I wrote intentions to pull myself to happiness on my bathroom mirror. No longer was it okay for me to focus on what I didn't want. I was going to get clear and navigate my ship back to happiness. The bottom gave me clarity and an authentic insight into the possibilities of living a fulfilling life. What I wanted was to be a writer, and I longed for exploration, adventure, and to be able to work outside and from anywhere in the world. I made it my full-time mission to become a travel writer.

Suffering through the depression and addictions sparked a deep desire in me to stop holding back and to start living a life that had real meaning. Luckily for me, I discovered the source of my unhappiness was the fact that I was ignoring my inner voice and refusing to ask myself, "What do I really want?"

I immediately took stock and redirected my future. I left my high-paying corporate job, sold almost everything, and moved out west. At first it was like teaching an old dog new tricks; I resorted to my safety zone of doing what was familiar. I took a job in marketing and the depression crept back in as I rotted under the fluorescent overhead lights. I would gaze out of the third floor window, and the trees that lined the streets would whisper to me, "Shannon, you don't belong in there, you belong out here with us in nature. Come play with the world." I started to use the job as a bridge to connect me to my future self. Who I wanted to be was more of a focus than who I was. I allowed myself room to be me, which included spending evenings and weekends with my writing self.

I pulled out and dusted off my magic bucket list and began to fearlessly check things off. I traveled solo to Paris and explored the culture and myself. After that journey I published many stories in inspirational books, like *Chicken Soup for the Soul,* and national travel magazines. It was as if the universe was winking at me, saying, "Welcome to the real you!" Sharing my stories with others seemed to not only open up a space inside of me that yearned to come alive, but also motivated others to have enough courage to follow their own hearts as well. By sharing my real self, I inspired others to be true to themselves, thus continuing my love affair with writing and sharing my experiences to help others find their inner light. For the first time in my life, I was leading with my heart, rather than my head. Things started to flow more easily, and life didn't feel like such an uphill battle. I was in line with who I wanted to be rather than forcing myself to fit some confining role set up by society's standards, my parents' or professors' view of how it "should be."

Obviously, it was tough to leave a day job. All of the security wrapped up in working 9-5 had kept me in limbo for a couple years. I would long for happiness and felt ashamed for allowing myself to stay in an environment I couldn't stand.

That changed, of course, when I traveled. Every time I would go to another place, a spark lit up in me. The conversations I had were more enriching, and the beautiful earth would smile at me. I lived in a constant perma-grin state. It didn't matter that I was stuck in the middle seat on the airplane, lost my luggage or had to travel 12 hours by plane with dehydration, a hungry belly, and a migraine. It never mattered that I couldn't speak the local language or even read the signs. When I traveled nothing else mattered and I felt free to be me. Through my authentic, vulnerable experiences of life, I learned that happiness is not a destination but a state of mind.

I found that even when a situation seems dreadful or impossible to comprehend, it is an experience, and being present in the experiences, rather than removing myself and running away, is part of living a fulfilled life. Complaining keeps us from connecting to our true self and keeps us in the shadows of life. Feeling life is the connection to being happy.

Every time I travel, I am like a wild horse being released from captivity behind caged doors. Being able to roam and explore all the facets of the world, my heart is happy. I found my happy; for me it was cracked open through moving through the fear, depression, and anxious emotions to discover a world of wonder, adventure, authenticity, and raw aliveness.

Today, I travel, write, and explore the world and share my tips on finding lasting happiness through workshops, lectures, and on my website. I created the site playwiththeworld.com, an online destination full of inspiration, motivational tips, and foolproof tools to help others find their happiness. I receive messages from fans all around the world who are moved by my transparency. They share stories of recognizing their own courage and stepping into their true selves. There is nothing more rewarding for me than to see the impact I can have by being my true self and, in turn, seeing it inspire others to be real. By sharing myself with others, I find it gives all of us an opportunity to impact the world together as we move to a more transparent, honest, and loving place.

The message I share is not about travel. For me, travel is the catalyst for the bigger picture. It is about authenticity and purpose and living your dreams and being true to yourself so you can be of highest service to the world. That is what this book is about. I hope it will help you "Find Your Happy." My website and all of the work that I do is dedicated to helping others fall passionately and full heartedly in love with their lives. Through podcasts, lectures, audio downloads, vlogs, stories, and workshops I have seen the impact living our dreams can really make.

I feel I have found the pot of gold at the end of the rainbow . . . the happiness on the other side of fear is the pot of gold of life. And when you strike gold, you want to tell everyone. I want to share my happiness; my mission is to share this message with the world.

Life is always going to throw us curve balls and situations that "don't fit" or "work" with what we expect. Learning to see the beauty in all situations is what I do and what I want share. My work is much bigger than travel writing. When I tell people, I am a travel writer, often they are struck with envy, they'll say, "What an amazing job! I am so jealous! WOW! I wish I could do that." My answer is always the same, "It is amazing, and you CAN do it." You can do anything you want in this life. You can make the most out of every single moment. I am not saying let's all go out and be a population of travel writers. I recognize that people don't really want to be a travel writer, as much as they long for the sheer notion of stepping away from what is not working in their lives to follow their hearts and live a life they love. This is what is reflected in their eyes.

No matter where we go in the world, no matter how much money we make, what we own or how fat or thin we are, we all want the same thing – happiness. We all want peace and we all want to feel love. I teach people how to do that and that is what this book will do for you. I was able to pull myself out of a desperate situation into a state of constant peace and happiness, and so can you.

Travel writing is my happy, but this book is not about travel writing. It is not about galloping around the world, frolicking between exotic destinations to be pampered in the trendiest hotels. It is about exploration of self, loving allowance for others, and cultivating an awareness and compassion for one another so we can create space to allow ourselves to be free, to be 100% us.

Imagine never feeling guilt, fear, or loneliness again. This book is designed to help you remove the blocks that are keeping you from living your true self because when you do walk that path, you can't help but to glow from the inside out and authentically *Find Your Happy* from within.

Through my "All Clear, Take Off" approach, I share the tips and secrets I used to pull myself out of depression and into a place of pure love, excitement, and joy. By first clearing out space, physically, mentally, and spiritually, we create a clean, clear space for our dreams and goals to manifest into reality. Having happiness is not a challenge when we remove the blocks to happiness and seek it from within.

I spent the majority of my life looking for happiness out there — in a boyfriend, in a new car, a new promotion, or a gigantic loft. Whatever it was, I was always searching in the wrong places. It wasn't until I started to travel and experience life fully that I realized happiness is within us at every moment. Once I recognized this, my entire world began to shift.

My dreams started to come true faster. I was meeting wonderful people and I was more content and at peace with the world and myself. It all started with my dream, believing in it, and actively living each moment of my life. Every day is an adventure and my goal is to help others navigate their own life adventures. It is daring to take a stand for what you want, but we all owe it to ourselves to love life and to be fully happy.

I've come a long way from being stuck on a path that wasn't made for me. The tears of rage have never come back. I went through all of the addictions and the depression and emotions associated with being off track. I know how it feels to be stuck, to feel hopeless, and to ask yourself, "Is this all there is to life?" With a daily practice of setting intentions, clarity, and focus I have manifested an authentic life that is in balance with me. I am no longer living in fear or letting society tell me what I should or shouldn't be doing. Life is exactly what you want to make of it. Life is a precious gift and this book is my gift to you. For anyone who has ever felt off track or consumed by fear, worry or outrageous emotions, this book will help you learn to love life again.

My focus is to help people all around the world, through my writing, travel trips, personal coaching, group workshops, and lectures, to create lives that they are in love with. I offer tools, motivation, and courage to help people follow their hearts, play more, dream bigger, and start experiencing an extraordinary life! Are you ready to love your life fully? Let's dive in!

Introduction

Thank you for choosing a path of love and focusing on happiness. *Find Your Happy* is one sure step of getting you on track to love every single moment of your life. At this point you may be wondering what the plan is. The purpose of this book is to help you remove all of the clutter (mental, physical, emotional, even spiritual) that is keeping you from being all that you can be. The idea is to help you shine light on the areas of your life that need a little tender loving care. You will create positive change and love your life fully.

My journey of suffering through addictions and depression to find happiness has equipped me to guide you. Sharing my experiences with others through coaching, workshops, and lectures has given me the power to stand behind the methods shared in this book. What follows in these pages is the result of me digging deep to find happiness on the inside, rather than seeking it externally. I have spent years perfecting this method and guess what? It really works. When you believe you will achieve.

Through my "All Clear, Take Off" method you will begin to see shifts in your own life. The way you relate to people and the amount of energy and time you spend trying to make things happen will no longer feel like a chore. Life will flow more effortlessly and you will enjoy the entire ride. The beauty of "All Clear, Take Off" method is that it is the first book to really dive deep and look at all the areas of life that aren't working. If you are trying to detoxify, but your teacup is full of old tea, there is no balance or room for anything new. Naturally good and bad tea cannot come into your cup because it is full of bad tea. When you begin to remove the tea, chucking the things that don't work and getting rid of the drama and negative baggage, then miracles can happen. Sadness can turn into happiness. Opportunities can come to you and you can receive them. When the teacup is empty, you can put good things into it, like your hopes and dreams. You can invest in things that have value and make you feel good, but you must start with clearing out space. It is a mandatory approach that so many self-help books and happiness gurus skip over. Starting right now, choose to make a commitment to yourself. This journey is part of life and you have come to the best place possible to declare the start of the new you. Say goodbye to the depressed, sad, and scared you, because after you turn the page, the fun stuff begins. You will be in the driver's seat on the road to success in life.

Part One: All Clear

The book is divided into two parts. The first is "All Clear." "All Clear" is the aspect that helps you dig deep into the nooks and crannies of your life to help shine light on what isn't working. We will get real honest with ourselves. It will be fun, challenging, and rewarding. You want results, I am sure, and I am confident you will achieve them by starting with the "All Clear" method. Just as a plane must have safety checks before liftoff, you must do a spot check, remove clutter, and ask the tough questions to regulate your safety, because when you do take off it will be a big blast off.

Each chapter focuses on a separate issue connected to breaking through barriers and living your life fully. I will give you step-by-step guidance on how to apply each new idea. Please visit my website playwiththeworld.com for additional guidance. Each chapter also has an audio component called Motivational Mantras that you can find on my website, playwiththeworld.com, under Shop. Each chapter has a vlog to accompany its message, on playwiththeworld.com/vlogs or go to YouTube and follow *Play with the World* channel. In fact, there are many juicy goodies on the website designed to help you to stay connected to your happy before, during and after this process.

Each chapter is divided into mini sections to help you create lasting results. Each chapter starts with an inspiring quote; this will help get you into the mindset of what is to come. It always makes for an awesome feel-good moment to read positive things. In each section, I will share a technique, suggestion, and idea about how you can shift your perception and move towards happiness. Since this book is a guide about finding and keeping happiness, it is also structured as a workbook for you. Most chapters will have an Awesome Opportunity section, which is basically a chance to try it out for yourself. I called them Awesome Opportunities because you have a choice to do as much or as little as you see fit. It's like extra credit, and if you answer the questions in each section you will see great results in your own life. This book is a guide to help you break through barriers, so it is highly recommended that you do all of the work in order to get and keep your happy for good.

Part Two: Take Off

After you have done all the hard work in Part One and removed the clutter that has kept you from being the awesome shining you, you are ready to Take Off. When I say hard work, I am not trying to scare you off. Don't worry at all; it's not bad. In fact it's fun because you get to learn about yourself and you will learn what really makes you happy. You will be in a position to blast off and live your life fully present, excited, and full of love. The second half of the book contains suggestions, ideas, and ways to apply your happy in the world. By being true to yourself, your happiness will manifest into greater opportunities. The "you" at the end of this process will not be the same "you" sitting here right now.

Take a moment and step back from the situation and look at the "future you." What does she/he look like, sound like, and seem to know that you don't know? Look to the "future you" for guidance because that "future you" will be full of confidence, light, love, and acceptance. The "future you" is reaching out to help you take a step towards happiness. Are you ready?

Motivation: *Play with the World*

Throughout the book I will mention playwiththeworld.com. I set up this author blog site to help inspire others to love life fully. It is the sister site to this book, where you can go for complementary messages, vlogs, lectures, articles and motivational mantra meditation CDs. Everything on the site has been created for you to help you find lasting happiness. Visit the site and make sure to sign up for the free "Love Your Life to the Fullest" guide.

I will mention *Play with the World* and to the community of members and site often. *Play with the World* is more than a website, or a guidance portal — it is a mindset. *Play with the World* is a lifestyle and a community of like-minded people who believe in the power of self and following their heart. It is for adventurous souls who know there is more to life. *Play with the World* is a mission, a journey for all who seek everlasting happiness and want to love their lives fully. If you haven't already done so, make sure to check it out, so you are already familiar with it especially since I refer to it through the book.

Now that I have given you the nitty gritty we are ready to embark on the journey. Get ready for awesome you to come out and play!

Part One: All Clear

Clearing Space so Fun Can Be Effortless and Abundant

CHAPTER ONE

STRIP DOWN

"To become learned, each day add something.
To become enlightened, each day drop something." — **Lao Tzu**

Do you ever get to the point where your world is out of control, spiraling downward as you crash to the floor, flooding the tile with dripping tears? That was me just a short time ago. I was drowning in a deep depression and surrounded by chaos. Everything I did was uncomfortable. My relationships were superficial, abusive, and demeaning. My job was pointless and I couldn't look in the mirror and see anything good. One night I burst into such an intense burst of hysteria that I was forced to stop before drowning in my hot tears or suffocating.

I splashed water on my face, stood up and said, "I can do better than this." I looked around my ridiculously overpriced loft and saw clutter. I saw dirty, stained clothes that I hadn't worn in a couple of years; I noticed things that didn't represent me or the person I wanted to be. I grabbed a trash bag and started where I assumed it would hurt the most: the closet. I pulled out everything that wasn't working. I didn't know what else to do but clean, unclutter, organize and remove the crap that had piled up. All I really knew was what I had been doing had not been working. Albert Einstein famously said, "Insanity is doing the same thing over and over again and expecting different results."

Insanity had driven me to a static state of numbness piled high with stuff that didn't feel comfortable. It didn't take me long to recognize that my outer environment mirrored my internal state. Over the past years I had packed on 30 pounds by shoveling toxic sweets and deadly drugs into my body, mingling the process with obscene compulsions. I would trade one addiction for the next in search of my perfect potion, but it all left me feeling cold, abandoned, and lifeless. I was treating my body like a trashcan and it didn't take long to reflect in my outer world. As *A Course in Miracles* states, "Your outside world is a reflection of your internal state."

It was obvious that if I felt unloved, lonely, uncomfortable, and unworthy, then my home, relationships, and opportunities could only reflect the same. The process of starting fresh, getting back to basics, and stripping down was the first and most critical step to helping me to regain my life. It represented a declaration that I was in control of my life and choosing to embrace goodness. When we clean out clutter, it removes the blocks to every other aspect in our lives. It becomes a gateway to let more life in. Think about it. If you have a door that is blocked with junk, you can't open it. The same thing is true in an energetic sense. When we have emotional, physical and material trash piled high, it drains us, slows us down, and blocks us. So the first step to playing with the world and living life to the fullest is to strip down.

Clear Out Clutter

There is no escaping the fact that retail therapy is one of the most fun things to do on the planet. Gather up the girlies, get gussied up, buy new clothes and neat things to make us feel, look, and act prettier. All of this is fabulous until we get our credit card bill, but that's another chapter. Shopping is one of America's favorite pastimes, but what happens to all the stuff we buy? Don't get me wrong: shopping is rewarding and therapeutic but when anything is attached to the word "therapy" we should collectively take note. Retail therapy is shopping with the primary purpose of improving the buyer's mood or disposition. If we use shopping to escape, then we are hiding out behind the glass windows. Items purchased during periods of retail therapy are sometimes referred to as "comfort buys."

So what happens to all those comfort buys? This section is not about making us feel guilty for buying all those awesome treasures, but simply to recognize patterns that might be counterproductive to our ultimate goal of peace and happiness. In 1986 the *Chicago Tribune* wrote: "We've become a nation measuring out our lives in shopping bags and nursing our psychic ills through retail therapy." In 2001, the European Union conducted a study finding that 33% of shoppers surveyed had "high level of addiction to rush or unnecessary consumption." This causes debt problems for many and the results are particularly bad for young people.

Trust me, I love shopping, but I think Lao Tzu said it best, "To become learned, each day add something. To become enlightened, each day drop something." This brings me to the first rule of adding more fun into your life: Strip down to add more fun. I bet if you took a look at your closet you may find things that just don't fit anymore. I don't necessarily mean whether they fit in the physical sense; I mean whether they fit you, who you are as a person. We have all bought that crazy fun "item" we thought for sure we could pull off. We wore it once and felt so uncomfortable that it was immediately retired to the back of the closet. It's okay to take risks, but not all of us can pull off Lady Gaga's latest look. Step one is to go to your closet and remove all of the things that don't fit anymore, physically and/or emotionally. Seriously take time to try everything on and examine yourself in the mirror. Pop on some party pumping hits and strut around. If the outfit doesn't make you feel alive, vibrant, and comfortable, it gets tossed into the Goodwill pile ASAP.

I also have a rule: If I haven't worn something in over a year, it automatically gets tossed. The goal here is to make room in our lives emotionally, spiritually and physically. Cleaning out the closet is a very good tool to help us unclutter and reboot our lives. Every transition I've been in, where I felt stuck and trapped, I would ask myself, "What could I do right now to feel a little better?" Since I can control my own environment, I will unclutter it starting with things that aren't working. I will clean out my closet. Would you guess that every time I have done a deep, down and dirty clean, within a week I get some great news? One time it was a promotion, another time an offer to my dream job, and another the first date with a man who still makes my heart sing. If you don't believe me, try it. Clean out your closet and watch what happens in the upcoming weeks. You may be surprised how cleaning out your own living space clears out space in every other aspect of your life. More space equals more opportunity. Goodness gracious, let the awesomeness flood in!

The goal of stripping down and returning to basics is to help you feel lighter and more connected to your true self. When we are bogged down with stuff, it isn't just a visual distraction, but also an emotional drain contributing to our low energy. Start with your living space. A closet is the best place to start because we usually start and end our day there. When it is clean, organized, and up-to-date, our mood every day will reflect that.

No More Junk in the Trunk

This may seem obvious, but junk mail is junk. It fills our mailboxes with clutter and we feel stressed with all the extra "stuff." Usually when things come in the mail that we don't want, we just get rid of them immediately, but what about our email inboxes? As far as adding chaos to our lives, email is as big a culprit as it is a friendly pal on printed paper. Our overstuffed inboxes confuse, frustrate, and stress us out. How can you possibly have fun in life when you are trying to read an avalanche of email? I get over 50 emails every day from people and companies that I don't even know. Chances are, you probably do, too. It didn't take me long to realize the connection between my lack of time to do fun and fulfilling things and the amount of items in my inbox. The more messages I have, the less time I have to enjoy the day. I am too busy trying work my way through the junk email maze.

There is an easier way. I started to track how many emails I had each day (on average 75) and how many were from close friends, family, colleagues, etc. (maybe 5). Over 85% of my messages every day were unsolicited junk. When you sign up for a mailing list or click on that web ad or browse a new site to enter your info for a sweepstakes, that precious personal info gets filed into a system and then shared. You are now a target for marketers of new companies and organizations. How do we stop this madness? We smile and just say no to mail flow.

That's right it is as easy as saying no. Each time a marketer sends an email blast there is a way to stop it. Go into that email and at the bottom there is always a spot to click unsubscribe. As you do this you will feel a sudden shift in your own energy. You may find that you feel more free and expansive. It is a small and simple deed but it works wonders in our lives. The same goes for magazine subscriptions, email lists, mailing lists, organizations, and credit cards — anything that adds clutter to your life. Dump the extra stuff and you will feel less bogged down.

Organize Your Chaos

The importance of downsizing is significant. **Whenever you take a stand to unclutter your life and downsize, you are sending a loud and clear message to the universe that you will remove unwanted things from your life.** It may seem silly, but when you physically and mentally clear out space you have more room to play, laugh, love, and live. When we clean out our area and get organized, it makes us feel productive. When we feel productive, we feel good and balanced. The process of straightening up all the nitty gritty helps us get organized.

Being organized increases our prosperity. The process I am sharing with you helps you see what you have and don't have. It eliminates waste and increases abundant space. The best part is you don't waste money-buying things you already have, but can't find. You will suddenly see your bank account grow, and you will have more time and moola to play. These are all great benefits worth every second of diving into the dingy grime and clearing it out for good.

Organization is a form of reverence and respect — for the time, energy, and blessings you've been given. When we respect our living space and the information we allow ourselves to receive, we feel more vibrant and balanced. When our living space is clean we can feel serenity. We have more time to spend with our loved ones, and can appreciate each moment. The time we spend together is of a higher quality because we are less frazzled, with more peace of mind and more physical energy. So get gallivanting, gals and guys. Start cleaning or stripping down to feel pleasantly pleased.

Time Is on Your Side

William Penn said, "Time is what we want most, but . . . what we use worst." This saying rings true for many of my coaching clients, because it resonates with everything we do. Think about how often we say we want more time, but the moment we get more time, we misuse it, waste it or regret not making more out of our day. **Time is nothing but a moment, changing every second. It is up to us to make each moment count.** Ferris Bueller said, "Life moves pretty fast, if you don't stop and look around every once in a while, it could pass you by." Time wants to be on our side. It is our friend and is always rooting for us to keep going and make the most out of every moment. The beautiful part about stripping down and clearing space is you will have more time to do the things you love. When you learn to be aware of each moment and appreciate truly living in the moment, time becomes endless. Take a moment to think about your perfect day. What does it include? Where do you go? Who do you share your time with? These are all indicators of what is most important to you.

Begin to construct your life around what you value. If your perfect day includes spending time with your loved one, be specific: What do you do together? Are you cuddling in bed watching a 1940s movie marathon for eight hours, or does your ideal day start out with a high voltage jump out of plane as you skydive together and brush death? These are two very different scenarios, both very real perfect days for different people. You need to be specific. Maybe your perfect day doesn't include another person at all. Perhaps you are into nature, writing, or painting beautiful landscapes in oil on canvas. Whatever it is, the elements that pop up in your vision of a perfect day should indicate what you value most in life.

The goal is to take these things and build your days around them. If cooking is important to you, but you worry you don't have enough time to give it the attention it deserves, set time aside every week to cook. Invite your friends over for a meal, or cook for coworkers and bring that food into the office. When we make time to do the things we love, we feel more balanced and whole. You always have enough time, money and energy for what is most important to you. Focus on where you are spending your time and money, and if it is out of alignment with who you want to be then refocus. Simply change your routine and watch everything else fall into place. When we do things we love, time stands still as we actively participate in every moment. Life becomes more about enjoyment, wonder, and fulfillment rather than a chore.

We are in charge of our own lives and how we spend our time. You should never do something you don't want to do. Lives are incredibly short. If it doesn't feel right to do something then you have permission to not do it. Who cares what other people will think? If you choose to go off and travel for a year, some may say you are ignoring responsibilities, but if it is right for you, then go on. If you want to quit your job and join the Peace Corps, what is holding you back? You get to make the most out of your life and no one is in charge of your life but you. So what if others don't understand? They aren't you. Too many times people spend their time trying to please others, hoping to make them happy. We end up sacrificing ourselves. Internal resentments build into a burning resistance to future opportunities.

I know this from personal experience. I used to play Pollyanna Peacemaker. I spent all my time trying to make sure everyone was happy. The whole time I did this, I never asked myself if I was happy. When I finally got the courage to dig deep and peel back the layers, I saw that everything in my life wasn't working. I would bend over backwards to help others, but I was the one left in the shadows. I always gave away my power. I never put my own opinions in the mix. This made me feel weak, alone, and depressed. My time was never my own. I spoke the words I thought people wanted to hear in the cities I thought they wanted me to live in. I share my experience with you to hopefully shine light on areas in your life where you have been inauthentic. If you are always giving your time, your money and your energy to those around you, you cannot possibly feel fulfilled. If you don't fill up your own cup it can never spill over to really help others.

Awesome Opportunity:

1. Go to your email inbox and delete every message that no longer serves you or your path to happiness. Unsubscribe to messages/updates and magazines you no longer read.
2. Go through your closet and get rid of anything you haven't worn in over one year. Trust me you won't miss it. Donate it.
3. Update your picture frames. Chances are you haven't really looked at them in a few years. Put fresh faces inside of them. This refresh will reboot your entire attitude.

In a Nutshell:

1. Take responsibility for how you feel and how you treat yourself. If you don't like something about your life, then look inside yourself to see how it is a reflection of your inner state.
2. Take inventory of your life, your stuff and your relationships. Get rid of everything that isn't working.
3. Every day should be a perfect day. If its not, go back to your value list and add in more of your values and what you love.
4. The *Pursuit of Excellence* self-improvement series reminds us that you always have enough time, money and energy for what is most important to you.
5. Make every moment matter. When you appreciate the moment there is an infinite amount of time.

Additional Resources:

Audio Meditation: *Find Your Happy: Motivational Mantras*, Track 1, "Strip Down" (available on iTunes, amazon.com, and playwiththeworld.com shop).

CHAPTER TWO

GIVE IT UP

"Open minds lead to open doors." — ***Unknown***

Let Go

One constant in life is change: seasons change, our jobs change, our relationships change, and circumstances will always change. If we know change is inevitable, then why do we get so bruised up and bent out of shape when it happens? Over the years I've learned to look at situations with a little more ease and perspective. I've realized that change isn't something to be feared but rather revered. The best opportunities in my life have been direct results of changes. From the outside, some changes could have felt brutal, such as layoffs, illness, car accidents, etc. Each change in my life has had a specific role in helping me peel back the layers to see the bigger picture. **Nothing happens in life that doesn't help us grow and connect more closely with our true selves.**

If we spend our time worrying about every outcome, life cannot flow or happen to us. When we seek to control, grasp, and manipulate situations, we essentially hide from our true purpose and connection to ourselves. If our desire in life is to play and relax into fun, then we must learn to let go and embrace every change. When we are consumed with worry and fear about situations, we hold ourselves back from reaching our full potential. However, saying it is as easy as "letting go" and actually letting go are two different monsters. I can speak about this because I was the queen of grasping and thinking, "Hold on tight fellas, we are in for a bumpy ride."

Some years ago, I called home a giant timber brick loft three blocks south of the mighty Sears tower in Chicago, Illinois. Although I grew up on the west coast I thought it suited me to venture out into the great wide-open America and nab a good job. I lived in five cities over a period of three years, and that didn't at all seem odd to me. I worked at one of the most well-known and respected international advertising agencies in the world. I had a man who wanted to marry me and a giant paycheck that I had no idea what to do with. I would go on spending sprees or drinking binges, always using substances to unknowingly disappear behind. I was a mess. I refused to admit that I was depressed. Crying hysterically to sleep every night should have been a red flag, but like all the others, I just skipped over it in pursuit of happiness in denial. In every relationship, every city, every job I took, something was always missing. I would tell myself this is what I want; I need to work at a big advertising firm, but when I got the position, it felt shallow, empty, and wrong.

Life will always throw us curve balls, and it is up to us to play ball. We have an opportunity at every moment to flip things around. If things are not going the way you'd like them to, then choose your thoughts wisely and switch it around.

I was beyond miserable in Chicago. What I didn't realize then was that I was manipulating my life to be something I "thought" I wanted, but my true self, the authentic me, knew that none of that mattered. I remember coming home one night, so overwhelmed with tears of rage that I was debilitated. I was cold and shaking and I knew that the hard tile floor could no longer be a source of comfort. As I started to choke on tears of fear, anger and resentment, I did something radically different for me. I let go of the expectation that my life was supposed to be anything more than it was. Suddenly, a shift took over my body as I started to laugh. Pleasure could pop through the pain. It was in that moment that I realized that I was holding on so desperately tight to my life, controlling every last minute detail, that there was no room for organic growth or real fun to come in.

Letting go of expectations is the single most important thing we can do for our well-being. When I let go of expecting my life to turn out a specific way, I was able to release the pressure and relax into the rhythm of life. This, in turn, became the tipping point for my life to unfold naturally the way it was designed. After my midnight meltdown, I took stock of my life and started to see things the way they were, not the way I had "hoped" they would be. The dingy rose-colored glasses were off and I was becoming the person I authentically wanted to be.

I know a lot of people who say, *"When I have a house,"* or *"When I am married,"* or *"When I have kids,"* I will be happy. Best-selling author and my dear friend, Gabrielle Bernstein, calls this *"the when I haves"* When I have (whatever it is), then I will be happy. I rode this rollercoaster for almost 25 years and it didn't result in anything but a substance abuse problem and depressed bipolar state. Ditch the expectations and let go of how your life is supposed to turn out and you will be free. Life is supposed to flow and be natural. It is not designed to be an uphill hike every day of our lives. We aren't supposed to struggle 365 days of the year. The universe wants to give us all the things we desire but we need to do our part and let go.

Awesome Opportunity:

1. Think of something that you wanted to happen, and it came true in your life. (Example: A first date seemingly out of the blue, a new job offer, a child, etc.)
2. What did you do before the event to help or make it come true? (Most of the time we don't have to do anything to make things happen in our lives except just show up and be present to receiving opportunities.) Pay attention to the state of flow.
3. Think about the energetic state that you were in before this event came true? Were you calm, happy etc.
4. Pay attention to those feel good feelings and hold them longer to manifest what you want in the future.

Don't Hold on to Anything Too Tightly

We don't actually help circumstances by controlling, worrying or manipulating any situation. In my relationship coaching workshops I share the story of two types of people. Meet Joey. She is trying to meet a man and desperately wants to settle down with The One. She can't "start her life" until she meets a man to make her happy. She needs someone to make her feel good about herself. Joey is more comfortable in relationships than being alone and clings to the possibility of finding "The One" on every first date. She goes to Starbucks with the intention to meet the man of her dreams. This energy is attached to her as she scans the room and judges suitable partners. When she goes into situations with this intention she is setting herself up for failure. The expectation of controlling the situation cannot be met. It is the law of life. Like attracts like, so if she is desperate, in fear and waiting for something to happen so she can be happy, then life will return the desperate, fearful, and waiting energy. Outcomes may include people not returning phone calls, canceling first dates or not even meeting someone for a first date.

As long as Joey is hung up on the possibility of happily ever after tied to a "specific outcome" she cannot be happy ever after. It is an unrealistic hope that she can't control. She gets to the coffee shop and doesn't see any single men; she becomes frustrated because "the expectation" isn't met. She orders her coffee and the barista makes it wrong. He apologizes and she just gives him a dirty look, saying under her breath, "People can't do anything right," and pouts on her way out. Whether it is big or small, the expectation in her eyes is a failed attempt. When we put expectations on things we set ourselves up for feeling failure. Our happiness depends upon an outcome that may or may not happen.

Now meet Lynn. When the time is right, she is hoping to meet a man to complement her lifestyle. She is a busy person who loves doing new things and does them with or without other people. She doesn't wait for a man or her friends to go enjoy life. She trusts that everything is in divine order and lets life unfold in front of her. She doesn't hold on too tightly to anything and goes into situations, without expectations.

She knows what she wants and focuses on that despite whatever in her current reality is not working.

Lynn goes to Starbucks and the barista makes her drink wrong. She politely asks him to make the correction, and the barista starts to talk to her, simply asking how her day is going. The two end up exchanging phone numbers, and she gladly accepts the invitation for a coffee date. Because Lynn enjoys meeting new people and getting to know them, she has no expectations when they sit down for coffee. She doesn't judge him, or try to put him into a mold of what she thinks her perfect man should look, act and talk like. The two hit it off and five years later they are still together.

Joey was in such a catastrophic state of expectations that the opportunity to meet a man was blocked. Lynn knew what she wanted but didn't put expectations around it. She trusted the feeling of what she wanted, but not the "frame." We might be able to relate to one girl more than the other but most likely we have a little bit of both in us. I was Joey before I realized the glorious life Lynn lives. Lynn is vibrant, excited, and truly living life to the fullest — all because she learned to let go and let life flow.

Life Never Goes the Way We Planned

"Remember that sometimes not getting what you want is a wonderful stroke of luck." – Dalai Lama

Sometimes not getting what you want in life is the biggest miracle of all. It took me a long time to see the world this way, but now it makes much more sense. Rather than trying to manipulate my life into what I think I want, I have learned to trust that the universe always has a better plan. When I was in Chicago, I was living the life I thought I wanted based on expectations set forth by others and what I believed would be a successful life. When I got what I thought I wanted, I wasn't happy. Something was always missing. Only when I learned to let go and relax into life were things able to flow to me, giving me more of a chance to enjoy life and stay in a constant state of adventure and play.

When I was in Chicago, my life was completely different. Along with the rest of the media and country, I was drowning in mistakes and fear-ridden circumstances. The economy had quickly taken a nosedive and fear in the advertising world sprang to an all time high. Stocks were plummeting, homes were being foreclosed by banks, car companies yelled for bailouts, giant big name businesses were going under, and this meant my clients were cutting budgets. I did my best to ride the wave of uncertainty. Then the day came when I was laid off.

With the rest of the world in a state of outrageous uncertainty and chaos, I could have handled the situation one of two ways. I could have gone into a deeper state of depression and partied with that pity posse. I could have joined collectively with the masses and said, "Oh no, I can't get a job in this economy, no one is hiring and the world is ending." But instead I said, "Sayonara job I didn't *really* like anyway," and "Goodbye lifestyle and city I don't love anymore."

Soon I was living in Portland, Oregon, surrounded by more love than I ever imagined, working at a job I truly LOVED and living life to the fullest daily. It didn't just happen overnight. I had to continually let go and trust that the plans were unfolding the way they were supposed to. The truth is life never goes the way we think it will, ever. Change is the one constant we can count on. It is how we deal with change that determines our success in life.

A year later, I was working at a different company and I was laid off, AGAIN. I could have easily pitched a tent and basked in the self-pity of, "Oh woe is me, I have been laid off twice in one year. I suck. I am not good at what I do. The world hates me and every place I work will fire me." But instead I had a perma grin as they told me goodbye, because I knew that there were bigger plans for me. Letting go of what I thought I wanted was going to be the key to my happiness. For me, being laid off was indeed the biggest blessing of all. Sure, it was cleverly disguised as misfortune, but the truth is every situation in life happens to help us get closer to our true self. My true self didn't belong at either of those companies. Through both transitions in my life, I focused on what I wanted and trusted that things would work out for the best. I removed fear from my thinking.

When I lost a second job in less than a year, I went home with a smile and a secret saucy saying, "Everything is in perfect order. I am taken care of and I look forward to my future." That same day I applied for another job and within a half hour of sending my resume, I was invited in for an interview. Less than a week later I had a full time job with a company in a smaller city than Chicago—Portland, paying me even more than my Chicago salary. Rather than going to fear and self-pity, I chose love and hope, and the opportunity literally fell into my lap. All I had to do was show up and become present to receiving. I turned what could be considered a horrible thing into a blessing; both layoffs were a miracle that put me back on track to my true self. It came to me because I stayed positive, focused, and was open to receiving. Life never turns out the way we think it will, but if we let go of our expectations, it can turn out even better.

We Create Our Circumstances

Do you ever have moments of déjà-vu, feeling you have already experienced the current moment? Do you ever find yourself saying, "I can't get a break"? Perhaps your work life is a giant rut. You hate your job, but when you get a new one the same problems persist. What about your dating life? Maybe every relationship is a repeat of a past failed attempt at love. I had both of those problems. I hated my job and blamed the people I worked with for my unhappiness. When I left one job, after the honeymoon stage of the new job ended, the same problems popped up again. This happened four or five times before I started to recognize that something wasn't right. I wondered why my new boss acted the same way as my old boss. I felt like they talked down to me, disrespected me and made me feel unappreciated. My dating life was one for the records. I cycled through emotionally abusive men like it was my favorite hobby. One boyfriend yelled at me for crying. Another said I was gaining too much weight and looked pregnant so he was embarrassed to hold my hand. Don't forget the one who told me my breasts were too small and he would pay for me to get a boob job. Even though the new boyfriends and bosses were different people than the old ones, the same patterns followed me around no matter where I went.

I finally realized that the only similarity between all of these failed jobs and relationships was me. I was the common thread, not them. My ex-boyfriends did not know each other, but I knew them. They looked different and felt different, but treated me in the same way. I knew that like attracts like, so I needed to take accountability for what I was doing to attract the same "crap" into my life. If I was the one thing they all had in common, it was time I peeled back the layers of my life to look at what was really going on.

I asked myself why all of my bosses made me feel unworthy and bad at my job. I was shocked to realize that I felt unworthy. I never felt adequate or qualified for my job. Even though I knew how to do it and I was good at it, my ego would come in and try to belittle me. In relationships, I never believed I was worthy enough to be in a fulfilling romantic relationship. If I couldn't value myself or love myself, then how could the world love me back? The world will always reflect our inner state and in each reaction is always a lesson.

Life Gives Us Lessons

This might sound lofty but stay with me for a second and consider that every single person we meet, every single job we take, every place we live, every "problem" we encounter is a simple lesson to teach us something new. Essentially, if we don't get the lesson we have to retake the course. Life is a big classroom where we take classes in compassion, honesty, and forgiveness. When we look at it this way we start to not only take accountability for our own life, but rich fulfilling opportunities can also unfold and guide us to the next stage.

I was getting the same lessons over and over because, frankly, I was failing every "class." No matter what job I took, no matter what guy I dated or what city I lived in, the same "lessons" would prevail. I know this because as soon as I took responsibility for my own life a shift happened that changed my life for good. By changing my perception of myself and bringing more of a conscious awareness to my emotions I was able to shift my reality.

Suddenly, bosses were complimenting me and giving me more responsibility. The men who made me feel bad about myself fell out of my life, and I met a beautiful person who not only treated me like a valued, beautiful, special person but also loved all of my natural beauty and me. My current boss wanted to promote me and told me he valued my contributions every day.

So look at your life and see the lessons that keep recurring. I kept repeating the same patterns and approaching romantic relationships the same way again and again, expecting a different outcome. A change happened when I took accountability for my role in my life and recognized that there was a lesson to learn of.

The purpose of this book is to remind us about the entire beautiful world we live in and the opportunities that await us daily to play. I wish it were as easy as saying, "Just add more play into your life," but humans are complex beings. We have trained ourselves to believe that good things in life are worth fighting for, or good things come to those who wait. Although both of these mantras could be true, I prefer to practice play daily by allowing love and fun to exist at every moment. By taking accountability for our lives and the situations we are in, we can learn to adjust our strained thinking and allow life to flow.

If you think about life being a whole bunch of lessons, then we are in one giant classroom. What kind of student do you want to be? Let go of the type of student you were in school, this is life school and you get to choose how you want to participate. It actually becomes kind of fun to see life this way because we can approach it like a game. Every new challenge brings an opportunity to grow and get to the next level.

Think back to when you were in school and how necessary recess was for your well being. We looked forward to the mini breaks, the chances to play outside and live life in a state of play. In reality, nothing has changed. As humans, we still thrive on recesses and taking breaks from our lessons. Even when we were young the lessons didn't stop when we bounced around on the playground, or rubbed our hands into the earth. Those were all just more things to study. The beauty of this world is that it offers us a chance to play at every moment. Every single situation provides us a chance to see the world with more compassionate eyes and more loving open arms and thus gives us an opportunity to embrace the fun in every lesson.

In a Nutshell:

1. All change helps us grow.
2. Let go of expectations to let life flow.
3. Life never turns out the way we thought it would; it turns out better.
4. You can't change the world but you can change your view of the world. Real change starts with you.
5. Things don't happen to you, you create your reality.
6. Every situation, relationship and challenge is a lesson.
7. Taking time to play is a human necessity.

Additional Resources:

Audio Meditation: *Find Your Happy: Motivational Mantras,* Track 2, "Let Go" (available on iTunes, amazon.com, and playwiththeworld.com shop).

CHAPTER THREE

NO MORE DRAMA

*"You only lose what you cling to." – **Buddha***

Put Down the Pity Party

One morning, I noticed a homeless person holding up a handwritten sign that said, "Passing through, anything helps." He was surrounded by all of his belongings — one small duffel bag, a backpack, and an extra pair of tennis shoes with the soles half off. I couldn't help but wonder about the drama I felt when I woke up. Oh no, I would be late for work, rush hour traffic sucks the life out of me, my boyfriend never called me back the other night, I ate too much ice cream the night before and I feel gross this morning, I meant to get up early to work out today, but the snooze button got the best of me, the list went on. Seeing this homeless man, helped me put them into perspective. We will always have situations that cause us frustration, so putting our issues into perspective is important to living a fulfilled life.

One of Newton's laws of motion declares that "everything that happens has an equal and opposite reaction." If we react to a situation that occurs, we cause even more ripples of frustration, anger, and resentment. This chapter is about letting situations happen in life without reacting to them. When we detach from the emotional aspect of events that happen in life, we can have a more balanced perspective that will help us make more rational and focused choices.

I can speak from personal experience about the power of balance and keeping emotions in check. I was the person who reacted to everything (and I still catch myself doing this). When I was six years old, my older brother was babysitting me and he told me it was time to go to bed. I looked at him, slammed my foot into the ground and said, "NO." He gave me a few more minutes. About ten minutes later, he said, "Okay, now it is time go to bed." I yelled, "No!" Naturally, as the big brother, he sensed I might be taking advantage of him and he got stern with me. I didn't like that one bit. After turning profusely red, I started to cry and scream. My body became tingly with overwhelming emotions of anger, frustration, worry, and fear . . . all because I didn't want to go to bed.

Even as a young girl my stubborn personality trait was evident. I was not one to do anything I didn't want to do, and it was indeed my way, or the highway. I had worked myself up into such a frenzy that my brother began to worry. He watched my flushed red face puff up from the waterworks. I choked on my own tears. My body started to shake. He didn't know what to do to get me to stop, so he put a towel around me and hugged me. He put his body weight onto me to get me to calm down. He was trying to let me know I was loved. But the shock of my big brother lying on top of me was so shocking that I started to scream even louder and declare, "I am NOT going to bed!"

Each emotion fed off the next, like a lion attacking its innocent prey. Worry turned into fear, fear turned into anger, and so on. At this point I was just a body in the scene—Shannon had stepped out temporarily. The emotions were so strong that my rational loving heart was nowhere to be found. I was a wet, hot mess consumed with fear and tears of rage. Talk about being a drama queen . . . *all of this because I didn't want to go to bed.*

Eventually my brother learned to back away and let my emotions take their course. I had to process all of them before I could get to a place of peace. Getting to peace is a scary process if we are afraid to look at our emotions. How many times have emotions taken over and gotten the best of you? It is a guarantee that dramas will come in and out of our lives forever, but it is how we work through each situation that determines success in life. When we can feel our emotions we are able to let go of the hold they take over us. It is when we run from them and choose not to acknowledge them that our lives feel chaotic and stressed.

Simply sit with the feeling and say, "Okay, I feel stressed right now. Okay, stress, I see you. Let me move through you." When we hold on to emotions and don't process them, they turn into larger problems, sometimes even disease. It is important to be one with our emotions and stop blaming others for our unhappiness. We have the power to be happy. We choose. In every given moment you can choose a happy or sad thought. Only you have the power to be fulfilled and satisfied. It starts with a happy thought. We cannot blame the world for what happens to us. I understand that some pretty nasty things take place, but our thoughts govern our responses to the events in our world. We must take responsibility; whether we like it or not, we have asked for every single thing in our lives. If we do not like it, it is up to us to change it.

Release Resentment

Life is really short. The older we get, the more experience, knowledge, and wisdom we collect, and the shorter it feels. We will not be on our deathbed thinking about the toys we bought or the fancy cars we went into debt to buy. It will be memories of the people who touched our lives — family, friends, even a stranger we connected with in a random situation — that we will carry through eternity. Every person in our lives has a purpose to help us feel, grow and see ourselves in a new, more appreciative light.

I spent much of my life holding on to resentments from past relationships that didn't last. I carried a giant chip on my shoulder and made future predictions about men being cheaters and liars. I told myself lies to make my false generalizations seem more realistic. So, naturally, when a really nice man did come into my life, I would be so closed off I couldn't see all of his princely charms. It took me many years to learn that past experiences do not have to dictate our identities or future. Most of us borrow fear from the past and project it onto the future. By replaying the "boy cheated on me" drama, we continue to make ourselves feel right by attracting the type of people who would cheat on us. This may feel a little heady, but bear with me.

Think about a situation in your life that isn't working as well as you would like it to be. Perhaps a boss isn't giving you a raise. Your current relationship feels different than it used to. Perhaps you want something that you don't have. **One simple step is necessary to getting whatever we want in life: Release resentment.** If you are carrying around resentment towards your boss because your raise is overdue, the single best action you can take is to release your energetic hold. By simply letting go of the past, we are set free.

I spent ten years carrying around a resentment left over from a past boyfriend. Nothing particularly bad happened when we ended, but because things did not turn out the way I thought they would, I had resentment towards him and to all the men I dated. I thought because that one relationship ended that love wasn't real and could never last. I had such a large chip on my shoulder that it made it impossible for anyone else to get close. Then on a two-week personal retreat to Paris, it hit me. I needed to forgive him and more importantly I needed to forgive myself. As soon as I did that something miraculously shifted inside of me. I felt more at peace.

Forgiveness Will Set You Free

When we choose to see others in a loving way, we are more connected to our true self. When we walk around with resentment, we tend to push people away and create more stressful situations. People come into our lives to teach us about ourselves. Every person in your life is there to help you in one way or another. Buddha said, "Holding on to anger is like grasping a hot coal with the intent of throwing it at someone else; you are the one who gets burned." When we forgive people, they can be free to be themselves. When we forgive people, we feel less resentment and blockage allowing other opportunities to come into our lives.

Sometimes people do things that really hurt. Our natural response is to get angry. We may even feel justified in wanting to "get even" with anyone who inflicts injury on our family or ourselves, but revenge will only create more suffering. You will feel more empowered when you forgive a person for their ill will because all actions of hate are just a cry for love. When someone does something unloving or unkind, it is a simple cry for a hug. Most of the time things happen out of emotions that separate us from happiness. Jealousy, manipulation and sabotage are all ugly disguised cousins of fear. Fear dresses up in many hats, but it always does one thing to us: it makes us act in ways we don't normally want to.

Fear traps us in our own thoughts of separation. The endless rage, resentment, guilt, and anger drain the life out of everything we do. By learning to recognize fear and say, "No way, not today," we can step into the light and learn to use loving thoughts and forgive others who hurt us. We say hurtful words to loved ones when we feel threatened or feel wronged. We act out in self-abuse by overeating, overworking or over indulging on harmful substances rather than practicing self-love and appreciation for each other. Forgiving others is one of the most important things you can do to become happier. When you are happy you are not stuck in the past or worried about something someone else did to you because you know that it was never about you anyway. Would you rather feel angry, anxious, stressed, and frustrated, or happy, free, satisfied, and fulfilled? Choose to forgive and you will be able to love your life more fully.

It's Not About You

Most of us spend our lives trying to execute a perfectly crafted plan to appease other people, but forget to check in with ourselves. We assume that when our best friend doesn't call back that we did something wrong or that our boss won't give us a raise because they don't like us. Well, did your boss ever tell you he doesn't like you? Did you ever forget to call someone back? Many times things happen and we humans, with all the emotional cobwebs intertwined inside us, get caught up in the moment and assume it is about us. When things aren't going your way or you assume someone is doing something out of character because of you, use this hard and fast rule: **It is never about you. EVER.**

We have taught ourselves to take things personally. We are born into a loving light with family, friends, doctors and loved ones caring for our every need. They take us in with unconditional love, bathe us, shelter us, feed us, and love us. The whole world revolves around us.

Then something happens that makes us question our world. Mom and dad fight. We see a car accident. Our brother hits us and makes us see the other side of love. Whatever occurs, our worldview automatically shifts. We see things in a different light and because of our previous existence when the world revolved around us, we feel a sense of subconscious entitlement. We assume dad is fighting with mom because he is mad at us. We think that everything that happens is about us. My challenge for you is to look at life in a slightly different perspective. What if everything that happens is not about you but about them? People say and do things not because of you, but because of their own fears.

For example, I spent 15 years yo-yoing 30 pounds of weight — up, down, up, down. I had insecurities and addictions I pushed through. Not until now can I say I am comfortable in my own skin. I finally realized that it isn't about a number on a scale but who I am as a person. Are you doing good in the world? Are we making a difference? Are we generally good and doing no harm? It isn't about the size, shape, or the color of your eyes. What is inside us makes us beautiful.

In the spirit of it not being about us, I recognized some common realities in my relationship with my father. While I was growing up he would always make comments about my weight, subconsciously engraving into my mind that I was not good enough. Recently, I pulled out a pint of ice cream and started eating it for dinner. I left the guilt behind and enjoyed every second of that silky, sweet bliss.

Looking at my mouth full of vanilla chip, sugary ice cream, my dad said, "You're real serious about losing weight aren't you?" I could have easily taken this comment personally and gone into an even deeper self-destructive mood. I could have defensively shot back, but I knew that what he said had nothing to do with me. I responded, "Forget weight, I am serious about living and enjoying life!"

A lot of the time people say and do things that reflect what they fear. He was looking at ice cream as a bad thing and not an appropriate dinner. He was not really concerned about my attempt to lose weight but rather with his insecurity about losing his own excess weight. Life is what we make of it, and when we stay stuck in negative thought patterns because we are busy picking apart looks, comments, and reactions from other people we lessen our own ability to live life to the fullest.

Choose Positive Thoughts

The brain can only hold one thought at a time, so why not choose a positive thought? Living a life of bliss, joy and abundant success means focusing on the good rather than the ugly. Choosing to think positively is a step towards happiness. There are two types of people in the world: those that blame the world for their problems and those that blame themselves. Those that blame themselves are usually a little more positive, but if you blame the world for your problems you can still learn to see the world in a kind, gentle, loving light vs. a harsh, negative fear-based one. When we pick happy things to think about, we shift our outcomes. If you don't believe me, try it out for a week. Why not think about what you *want* rather than what you *don't want?* When we choose to focus on happy and good things, more happy and good things can come to us. When we focus on things that aren't working or negative things we don't want in our lives, we tend to get more of what we don't want.

Awesome Opportunity:

1. Focus on an area of your life that isn't working as well as you would like.
2. Ask yourself (be honest) what you have been telling yourself in your head about this situation. What story have you been replaying?
3. Is this story true? (Most likely the story is NOT true. Did your boss really tell you he doesn't like you? Did your best friend really say you are fat? Etc.) Now that you recognize the story is not true, what benefits have you been getting by believing in the story? Do you get to be right, are you empowered, etc.?
4. Are you willing to let go of that thought pattern and start to tell yourself another story? For example, rather than saying no one wants to date you because you are fat, simply start by saying. "I have fabulous gifts to offer a significant other. I am an outstanding cook, lover, friend," etc.
5. **TRY IT OUT:** When the negative thoughts creep in, slap them in the face and start to say your new positive mantra.

In a Nutshell:

1. We are responsible for everything in our lives. Love it or leave it, but don't complain about it.
2. At the end of our lives we will remember the relationships we had and the people who touched and inspired us.
3. Forgiveness is important in helping you live your life to the fullest.
4. Don't take things personally because it is not about you. It is about them and their insecurities.
5. Think positively and more opportunities will come your way.

Additional Resources:

Audio Meditation: *Find Your Happy: Motivational Mantras*, Track 3, "Release Resentment" (available on iTunes, amazon.com, and playwiththeworld.com shop).

CHAPTER FOUR

CLEAR YOUR FEAR

*"Man cannot discover new oceans unless he has the courage
to lose sight of the shore." — Andre Gide*

Recognize the Little Voice in Your Head

According to Charlie Greer, The National Science Foundation reports that the average person thinks about twelve thousand thoughts per day. A deeper thinker puts forth fifty thousand thoughts daily. Most of us don't even realize these thoughts are going on. But the little voice inside our heads is the number one reason we stay safe in life. The little voice, often called the ego, is engaged in non-stop running dialogs. The conversations usually focus on judgment, under-appreciation or condescending tones. Rhonda Britten, founder of the Fearless Living Institute says people fall into two categories. Some blame the world for their problems; others blame themselves.

Depending on which category you fall into, your running internal dialog may differ. It is important to recognize what the voice is saying. Most of us go through life thinking that the little voice in our heads is "us" and that is why things are the way they are. But the reality is that voice inside our heads is not us. We do have control over what the voice can say. We can choose positive thoughts and loving intentions. Rather than judging other people or feeling insecure or jealous, we can remind ourselves to choose better thoughts. This practice will generate tremendous results in your life. The first step is to recognize that this voice exists, and it tells you things about yourself, about the world, about your past, and things that aren't true. Most the time the voice creates stories that feel real but are not real. *A Course in Miracles* states, "Fear is nothing but an illusion of separation." This essentially means that fear is simply something we create in our heads to try to protect us. Every person on the planet has the little voice. So, first recognizing that there is a little voice, and then understanding that everyone else is playing the same warped fear game can help make the next couple steps easier.

People often find that going with the flow and sticking to the normal is the best way to live life. The security of the steady paycheck, the ability to plan for the future and stash hordes of money away so we can play at the end of our lives is what society has conditioned us to abide by. Most of us travel through life feeling a little pull that we were meant for more, but ignore its push. My nudge was a tiny voice that kept saying I didn't have to sit behind a desk 40 hours a week to make a living. "What if there was another way?" I asked myself this three years ago when I hit the first of my three rock bottoms. I said, "There has to be another way. This 9-5 doesn't work for me." I immediately took myself on a me-retreat and dove into personal reflection. I asked, "What is going to make me happy?" I started by dissecting every single thing in my life ranging from my relationships to the clothes I wore. I rearranged my life and got rid of everything that wasn't working, including people that weren't working.

Take a Me-Retreat

There is only one person in the entire world who knows what will make you happy: you. Most people race around without stopping even to ask themselves, "What do I want?" I lived on that roller coaster until traumatic emotional pain made me get off. I moved from city to city on a mission to find my happy. I took the best jobs in the hippest cities to prove to myself that I was worthy and could do what it takes to be successful and happy. But none of it felt like me. I was always being someone I wasn't. I thought I wanted to lived in a giant loft in downtown Chicago, but I found that my happy could be in a little bungalow in the South Pacific spending less than $20 dollars a day. Simple is better for me, and usually the simpler we can make our lives the more we can make room for what is really important to us. So take yourself on a mini me-retreat. My mini retreat has lasted many years and will always be part of my life because I have learned that putting myself first is the essential ingredient to loving my life to its absolute fullest. How did I do this? I started with a list of simple questions that I never thought to ask myself before. Once I sat down and got honest with myself I learned a great deal. This process helped me cure my own depression and move towards a blissful, unapologetic exciting life.

Awesome Opportunity:

1. What five things do you value the most in life?
2. If you won the lottery and had a limitless amount of money, what would you do with your day?
3. What are the top three things you want to do during your life? (See more about creating a magic list in Chapter 7.)
4. What have you always wanted to learn?
5. What have you always wanted to have?

Most likely, after answering these questions, you will have a clear focus on what makes you excited in life. The trick to feeling fulfilled is to align your life with what matters most to you. For the five things that you value the most, make sure you incorporate at least three of them into everyday and all five into every week.

I looked at my list and poked at the holes. Not long ago I was sitting at a desk job, not enjoying nature, travel, or expressing myself. Naturally I was out of alignment with who I really was. If you feel like your life is off track or there is an area that is not working, ask yourself what you value and how you are incorporating that into your day. Chances are what you value is not present in the areas where you are struggling. When you make a value list, the things that are most important to you will rise to the top. The next part is simple; you simply incorporate what you value into your daily regimen. If you value family, then do not read the newspaper at breakfast; sit with your loved ones and listen, laugh, and love them. Turn off the TV at night and play with your friends, children, or pets. If you want to travel but worry about money, then focus on saving money vs. spending money. (More about making the most out of money in Chapter 6.)

The answer to the second question what you would do with your time if you had a limitless amount of money clearly reveals what is really most important to you. If what you answer in this second question does not include the five things you value the most that you listed in the first question, then you have a disconnect. What you do with your dream day should naturally incorporate every single one of your values. If it doesn't, take a look again and get honest with yourself and look a little deeper. When we make a list, our subconscious goes to town and begins to craft ways to make it happen. (More on setting goals and making life rock every second in Chapter 7.)

Part of my mini retreat was taking a vacation with me. I took myself to the movies by myself; I saw a movie I always wanted to see. I took myself to the ice cream parlor and ordered my favorite flavor. I left guilt behind and enjoyed me-time. I took a hike in nature and reflected on all the great things in life. I spent time with me. Part of a mini me-retreat is to take time out for you. If you feel more fulfilled, you can be there for other people; but make sure the people in your life are worthy of your awesome self.

Surround Yourself with Fearless People

Almost everyone has a "social vampire" in his or her life. Social vampires suck the energy out of you when you hang out with them, and make you feel icky when you leave. As part of my deep cleaning, I looked at all my relationships and thought about who made me feel good, supported and excited to be around. Who was dreaming big and interested in solving problems vs. talking about them? Those people who made me feel bad about myself, who didn't support my goals or left me feeling cold and bored, I chucked to the curb. It seems harsh, but I had to find a way to keep my distance. I stopped returning their calls and slowly weaned them out of my daily life.

Many times social vampires find their victims when they are down and in the dumps. When I was depressed, the majority of my friends were substance abuse addicts, depressed and negative people. I wanted so much to be a positive influence that I tried to stay strong and remind all of them that it gets better if you just believe and stay positive. Misery loves company and eventually I found it easier to join the dark side and complain, judge, and worry about things that didn't really matter. I joined forces because it was easier than going upstream and against the grain. Whenever I would provide a positive nugget they would laugh and say that I was naïve and stupid. I felt ashamed of myself, and didn't realize that I was a becoming a product of my environment. I grew up a happy, positive girl, but the more I hung around with people who didn't think highly of themselves and blamed the world for their problems, the more I lost myself. They wanted me to be like them, they wanted me to stay stuck in fear. My inner self kept screaming at me, "This is not you! You need to be yourself." I broke away, and a group of them even started an "I hate Shannon" club. People who I thought cared about me suddenly began spreading rumors and hate messages about me. Through this process I had to realize that **it doesn't matter what other people think about you. As long as you follow your heart and you are being yourself, then you are living a life of integrity and honor.**

Part of making the most out of life is to dig deep into yourself, your life, and your dreams and uncover the areas that aren't working as well as they could be. It starts with you looking inward. The people I called friends were not really my friends; they just felt safer when they had someone else to complain with. As soon as I removed myself from the toxic emotion sucking vampires, I found my productivity, self-esteem, and my opportunities expanded. My quality of life immediately bumped up and I felt more content and happy.

You may be wondering how on earth you are going to remove negative people if they are your best friends or family members. You can always do what I did. I set an intention at the beginning of each conversation. I said, "I will only hold space for happy, awesome thoughts. I want to hear about the good things going on, your goals, and how I can help you reach them. The moment you complain or start to judge someone or something I will have to hang up." Most of them got the message pretty quickly. What I noticed was that the "friends" who only wanted to gossip and talk dirt about their lives stopped calling me. They didn't want to talk about goals and were more comfortable complaining about situations vs. trying to solve them and learn from them. The people who were inspired and interested in making the most out of life called me more. Our relationships became so much more rich and fulfilling, just by sharing ourselves with each other and holding space for support, growth, and opportunity.

You may be asking who I surround myself with now. The people in my life are my power posse. They support me, lift me up, and challenge me to think even bigger. They always have my back, and I do the same for them. They take risks and show me what is possible in life. We have an opportunity in life to make every second fantastic and it starts with you and your friends. Surround yourself with positive, supportive people and you will immediately see the quality of your life expand.

Worry Is an Ugly Cousin of Fear

Many social vampires are just stuck in fear. They worry about the unknowns, they think about what could or couldn't happen, and they worry the life out of every situation. You don't have to be a social vampire to be a worrywart. There is a reason worriers are called worrywarts. Because worrying is a nasty ugly bump in your life. Worry makes things seem worse than they are. Worry is an ugly cousin of fear. Worry was my middle name a few years ago. I worried about everything from what drink I should order at Starbucks to why my boss hadn't said good morning. My entire life revolved around the tight knot clenched in my chest. I was anxious, scared, and saturated in fear. Fear is just our mind's way of saying, "Whoa! Watch out! Danger ahead, uncomfortable things approaching." Fear can actually help us make better choices. Fear is synonymous with the little voices in our heads. When we hear them we can choose to listen and believe them to be true or to say, "Thank you for your input but I would like to not listen to you. Fear, please go away."

Worry makes it harder for us to recognize what is driving our lives. Many of us see things happening out in the world and we take it all in and worry about our safety or future; our "right now" is consumed with deprecating, fear-based thoughts. One solution is to turn off the media. I am serious. I do not watch TV news, or read about it on the Internet. Our media spotlights fear-based reactionary stories: natural, financial and political disasters, violent crime, dismal forecasts, and distressing exposés. The media is a huge contributor to our internal dialog. We refuse to let our children take the school bus because we fear the unknown pedophile who kidnapped a child five years ago.

A great quote I came across by an unknown author is, "Worrying is like praying for what we don't want." Yuck, who wants to do that? Are you "praying" for what you don't want? We worry about potential people and what they might or might not do. Worry becomes the everyday vernacular. We stick together with our collective consciousness of worry. But what if there was another way to live? What if we removed worry from our lives and learned to embrace the unknown? What if worry became a signal of opportunity? Instead of worrying about a situation, we can learn to embrace it and accept it fully. Worrying about something doesn't change anything except your current state. Worrying makes us feel separated, anxious, and stressed, but if we shift away from this emotional state we can bask in love, joy, and abundant excitement. When I feel myself start to worry now, I confront it and ask, "Why are you worried?" Almost every time I am able to see that the worry is just a barrier between where I am now and where I really want to be.

For example, I stayed in advertising, behind a desk job three years past the time I knew I didn't want to be there, but worry of the unknown kept me there. My fear was, "How will I pay my bills if I quit?" I worried about the future and the giant sea of the unknown. This worry consumed me and kept me unhappy. It was really just a red flashing light into an unknown territory. The truth is, I had never ventured into the great big world of being your own boss. I knew I wanted it, but it was new and foreign to me. Naturally, from where I was sitting, it was a long haul to get to where I wanted to be: a self-employed, full-time writer. I knew what my dream was but worry stopped me from getting it. I finally took a stand for myself and punched through the worry. When I got to the other side of my fear I realized it wasn't nearly as bad as my little voices had cracked it up to be. In life, **risks are not as scary once you take them.** Once I took that leap into the unknown I recognized a new me. For the first time in my life I had peace with myself. I felt abundant, excited, and alive. Fear and worry have a funny way of obstructing our dreams. Once we recognize their purpose we can bust through them and love every second of our lives.

A few months ago my 92-year-old Grandma was sitting next to me, and I recognized that her reality was much different than mine. Here was a woman who has lived through the Great Depression, World War II, the Civil Rights Movement, Cuban Missile Crisis, the assassination of President Kennedy, 9/11, and now witnesses the administration of the first black president. But there she sat, with a soft subtle glow. Grandma always smiles, and she had a peaceful spark in her eyes. It occurs to me that my mini dramas, the self-loathing, and worrying about my next assignment are rather superficial in comparison. I asked this beautiful woman, "In your life, how did you get through the tough times?" She looked over at me and simply says, **"Well it all works out in the end now doesn't it? There is no point in worrying when things always turn out fine."**

Use Fear to Propel Yourself Forward

Fear will never go away. It is as much part of the human condition as the skin on our bodies. We will always have little voices in our heads, and fear will always pop up in some way. Many times it changes form. Whether it dresses up in stress, anxiety, or worry, fear is an indicator of stepping out into new territory.

People who take risks are generally more fulfilled and joyous in their lives. Many studies have been published that conclude people who push through their fear are a bit more intellectually curious, more self-aware, and even a bit happier than those who do not. If you want help pushing through your fears, visit playwiththeworld.com, a community of adventure buddies who are all living life to the fullest.

Awesome Opportunity:

1. Call a fearless friend from your past who has been on your mind and whom you have not talked to in a long time. Have a conversation with them.
2. Share your goal/value list with your number one supporter. Encourage them to create their own list and delight each other by entertaining the possibilities of tomorrow.

In a Nutshell:

1. Choose positive happy thoughts to get what you want.
2. Take a mini me-retreat. Take time for you so you can be there for others.
3. Do what you love every single day.
4. Get rid of people who suck the life out of you and surround yourself with happy healthy people.
5. Don't worry about what other people think; always be true to yourself.
6. Don't let worry creep in and keep you playing small.
7. Risks are not that scary once you take them.
8. Let go of worry, because in the end everything always works out.

Additional Resources:

Audio Meditation: *Find Your Happy: Motivational Mantras,* Track 6, "Choose Love Over Fear" (available on iTunes, amazon.com, and playwiththeworld.com shop).

CHAPTER FIVE

LIFE IS A GAME,
ARE YOU PLAYING IT?

"What you are is what you have been.
*What you'll be is what you do now." — **Buddha***

Stop Watching, Start Playing

Even though life is sometimes messy and unpredictable there is one constant — opportunities will always come and go. When we are open to new things and eager to branch out of our safe and cozy comfort zone, we can open up a world of new possibilities. It all starts with one easy step. Play the game and get on the court. Landmark Forum's self-improvement course teaches people how to build their best life and the power of getting on the court in life vs. sitting in the stands.

Think about a sporting event. Spectators cheer from the stands but never put themselves at risk. They are not the ones making anything happen. Rather they sit, watch, judge, and wait, while the players are full of life. They are the doers making the game happen and work with them. They see an opportunity and go for it. They take risks and play hard. Of the two types of people which would you rather be?

More often than not I have been a spectator in my own life. I let life happen to me and fell into deep, moldy holes. The only way to pull me out of each episode of depression was to take responsibility for my own life

39

and start making calls, literally getting my butt up out of Self-pity Ville and taking action to guide me in a better direction. It started by taking one single step forward, by getting on the court of my own life.

If you look at your lives as a best-selling book, or blockbuster movie, how is yours playing out? What kind of picture are you in? Is it full of depression, mistakes, regrets, and secrets? Or are you the hero in your own starring role? Are you in a role that challenges and excites you? Do you seize the day and make the moment matter? The opportunity here is to dream of possibilities beyond the traditional confines of cultural and social acceptability. Whenever there is an area of our lives that we are unhappy with, the human tendency is to ignore it and simply act as if it is not an issue; out of sight out of mind.

For example, maybe you are unhappy with your job. I was the queen of bitter job certainty. I lived the "this is how things are" card to its death, meaning I was a victim of the negative perceptions of my job. I worked with people who didn't understand me or respect my contributions. They always made me feel like an outsider, and I always had a boss who seemed to have ulterior motives. I could never trust them. No matter what city the job was in, this was the way I perceived my job. I'd quit one company and start working at completely different companies, sometimes even different industries, and would always find myself crying in the bathroom on lunch break.

I would tell myself it was normal to cry at work and this is just how life is supposed to be. I would come home and complain to whoever would listen about how bad my job was, how lame the people I worked with were, and how I wasn't getting what I deserved. That's a lot of "me, me, and me" talk if you ask me. I was pretty self-consumed and exhausting the victim role. I kept playing out my same reality over and over; One day I was talking to a friend, I was complaining about my new boss and the work I was doing, when she gently said, "Sounds like your last two jobs."

I realized then and there that the only thing all these nasty, toxic environments had in common was me. I was the connecting thread to all of these mishaps in the workplace. I took mental stock and realized I was accountable for everything in my life. All of these patterns that kept surfacing were a common thread of my life, not theirs. I asked myself, "What have I been doing to create this reality?" Quite simply, I hadn't been getting on the court or playing a starring role in my own blockbuster. I had been letting life happen to me vs. co-creating with life and being accountable for my own actions and patterns. These patterns were really an inner cry for help. I kept living the same reality of moving between jobs, states and countries to get away and start fresh, but I wasn't able to look at the big picture. No matter where I went, these patterns would keep recurring until I learned to recognize each situation as an opportunity to learn something new. Each new job was a lesson, and the lesson would keep coming up until I recognized it and greeted it full-heartedly.

Is there a situation in your life that is causing you frustration? Challenge yourself to look at the situation with fresh eyes and ask yourself, "What is this situation trying to teach me? What can I learn from this?"

Until I took full responsibility for my spectator role I would continue to be a victim of my own life. What I wanted was a change. I needed a break from the draining existence of letting life happen to me. I immediately took stock of my life and realized what wasn't working must change. No longer was I in a position to ignore it or act like this was just part of life. I knew I had the power to change things and make my life better. If I wanted a happily ever after, then I needed to start with a happiness makeover.

Get a Happiness Makeover

Life is what we make of it. If we are bored, depressed, sad, or lonely, we have the power to change it. Every part of your life that isn't working is a place to shine light and let love in. I couldn't stand my job. No matter where I went, which job I took, the same unhappiness followed, until I gave myself a happiness makeover. A happiness makeover is just a simple way to look at life with a fresh perspective. I started by taking stock of what wasn't working. I sat down and made a list of what I wanted, not what I didn't want. Most of the time people get bogged down in what we don't want rather than focusing on what we do want. Life is a magical journey to a wonderland of fun, fulfillment, and utterly extraordinary happiness, but we can never get there if we don't declare what we want. We will continue to get what we don't want if that's what we focus on.

That is why I kept meeting up with the same boss in different jobs. If we shift our minds to focus on what we want we will see a shift in our reality. If you don't believe me, try it out for a week, just seven days. See how your world reflects your inner thoughts. If you still don't believe me and think this is hocus-pocus, then ask yourself, "What isn't working in my life? What have I been telling myself?"

For me, one area I was unhappy with was my weight. I was overweight and struggled with feeling secure about myself. I would go on spurts of eating a very healthy diet, counting calories, and working out daily, but every time I looked in the mirror, I would see blubber and the fat kid who was bullied from third grade on, who used food to block her real feelings from the world. I couldn't say, "I love you," to my reflection in the mirror or even say, "I am beautiful." It was next to impossible to lose weight through this process. I would scream and yell because my actions so clearly should have been achieving better results, but the problem wasn't my actions, it was my thoughts. My thoughts about myself were so overpowering that they would take me on a wild roller coaster and stay situated in fatville. The truth is I wasn't even that fat, but our ego mind plays nasty tricks, manipulating our reality.

It wasn't until I started to look at what I wanted, not what I currently had, that I saw a change. Sure I was overweight and felt uncomfortable in my skin, but I had to move past my current reality to get to a place of peace. **I have to accept what is, in order to get to what I want.** I started to look in the mirror and say nice things to myself. "I like the way you did your makeup today, Shannon." Or "Your nose looks really pretty." I had to start small in order to move the process forward. I would picture myself in smaller size clothes and celebrate all of the wonderful things I did for myself. "I drank green fresh juice for breakfast," "I worked out today." Rather than beating myself up mentally for eating the cupcake at work or only working out for 30 minutes, I would say thank you to myself for the kindnesses I did for myself. Soon enough my world started to reflect my intentions. I found the weight naturally fell off and I was able to see the power of setting an intention and focusing on what I want.

The same applied to my work situation. I was unhappy with work and consumed with what I didn't want. I would say, "My coworkers don't like me or understand me. I feel like I can't do anything right; my boss doesn't appreciate me." I sat down and made a list of what I wanted. I pulled out a giant white board and big black marker. I wrote, "I want to work with like-minded people who love, respect, and appreciate my skills and me. I am paid what I am worth and eager to go to work every day." I adopted this mantra and played it in my head on a daily basis at work. When my boss would say something that felt demeaning I simply smiled and said to myself, "I work with like-minded people and love where I work." I did this for four days. On the fifth day, my boss called me in and said, "This isn't working out. We need to let you go."

I smiled at them and left immediately knowing in my heart that everything was in perfect order, because I had taken responsibility for my own life. I knew I didn't want to be there anyway. The people and the work were not in line with who or what I wanted out of a job. I pushed all worry and fear away and continued to recite my mantra. I came home that day and noticed an online ad for a job at a different company that looked like a perfect fit. I applied, not thinking much of it, as I had applied to over 50 jobs in the past few weeks. Within one hour, the creative director asked for an interview. One week later, I had a full-time job, with everything on my list and more. For the first time in my life, I worked with like-minded people, who valued, appreciated, and cared about me. Every morning I would go to work, which didn't feel like work, because at the time I loved what I was doing. All of this happened when I shifted my mindset to focus on what I wanted, not on what I currently had. By doing this I was able to change my work and create a happy place where it was once dark. I did all this by getting on the court and playing an active role in my life. Getting a happiness makeover is as simple as looking at the world as a glass half full, and focusing on what you want vs. what you don't want. Something as simple as a smile can help, as smiling more will always do the trick.

You Are More Beautiful When You Smile

"Because of your smile, you make life more beautiful." — *Thich Nhat Hanh*

The world is a better place when you smile, and smiling is a form of appreciation, love, and gratitude all rolled up into a pretty little package. **The best gift you can give to yourself and the world is to lighten up and smile a little more.** Think about smiling, and your mood when you see someone smiling. When we smile our brain releases endorphins, which are a chemical hormones linked to euphoria. Yes, that's right, **smiling is the closest thing to heaven on earth, and we all have the potential and power to do it more.** No matter how desperate or sad our current state, we can smile more. Making a daily practice of smiling will improve our mood, our outlook on life, and our quality of life.

When I was in a deep depression, I knew I had hit rock bottom. I decided to do a little experiment because in all honesty there was only one direction I could go after being so low and that was up. The only thing I could do was find it in me to make my mouth turn upward. A simple crack in the lips turned my devastating frown into a gentle smile. Even when I was crying and stuck in a dead end, I asked myself, "What is one thing I can do right now to feel a little better?" I would force a smile, and the mere act of bringing my lips upward made my mood shift. I would lighten up a little and feel my body release tension. It was easy for me to fake it until I made it. I admit at first it seemed silly and I didn't know how it would make a difference, but in time my smile became real and a kind reminder to myself that life doesn't need to be as hard as I perceived it to be. I can simply smile and remind myself to just be in the moment and feel the moment. When we smile, we are more beautiful, more approachable, and more adept at taking on any situation. People who smile often usually are happier than those who don't smile. The trick is to surround yourself with things and people that make you happy and smiles will flow abundantly. There is no need to force smiles if you are genuinely in a happy state.

Forcing a smile was a way for me to get out of my own way and try to turn a dark situation into a lighter one, but after time it became natural. There are really different aspects of smiling that we can apply to our lives at any time. Right now, smile. Do it as you read these words. How do you feel? As I wrote this sentence I smiled, and pure joy flooded through my body. I felt my mind ease up, and my body felt lighter. A smile is the kindest thing we can do for ourselves, and it's free. We can share it with the world. It is perhaps the best gift we can give to the world.

Smiling is a simple thing we can do to not only help us feel better, but help us connect with others too. It is the experiences and people we meet along the way that make life so rewarding. Part of finding your happy and living life to its full capacity is to experience rewarding relationships. I lived a large portion of my life denying myself personal relationships because I was afraid of getting hurt. I would reject potential love interests by finding reasons not to like them. Men would continue to ask me on dates and I would get involved with guys who I didn't have intimate feelings for because I was so scared of losing love if I found the real thing.

The funny thing is by pushing love away I was creating an isolated vortex of depression, loneliness, and self-sabotage. I didn't realize this was what I was doing, but fear was driving my outer world. Looking back on all of it now, I realize my depression was a catalyst of my denial of love. I pushed love away, but at the core of every human is a drive and need to give and feel love. Every single person in this world craves love. The emotions of life, of love lost, of needing to be connected to another all stem from the heart and our ability to make other people feel important. When we choose love over fear, our lives are richer, deeper, and more enriching.

When I decided to approach my romantic relationships from a place of love and kindness vs. fear and denial, I opened up an entire world of grand opportunities. Many times people choose to play small by staying in fear-based thought. We create barriers to potential connections to other humans. We go about our day living in a bubble. Poor thoughts become our world. We think our spouse has fallen out of love with us because our biggest fear is feeling alone. We pretend our lives are crafted perfectly to make sure we are safe and secure, but what we do by refusing to let love in is refusing life. Love equals life. Choosing fear-based thoughts is essentially choosing to be alive, but not live. Everybody dies, but not everybody lives. A little exercise you can do to see the power of connection is to simply focus on your interactions. By living each day with an intention to make a difference and connect with another person you will open up grand opportunities in your life. Everybody wants to feel heard, so we can start by listening more. Listening to another person is sometimes the simplest act of love. By being present and focusing on someone else, we can help in ways deeper than we can ever imagine. Sometimes just getting out of your own bubble is the best way to brighten your day.

Connection is Key. Everyone Is Just Looking for Love.

Human connection is the single most important thing for every single person on earth. Everybody just wants to love another, to be loved and express love. So it is essential that we make the most out of our lives by expanding our hearts and hugging love when it comes around. Too many of us walk around in a shell running from love, without even realizing we are hiding ourselves from bliss.

I spent the past 15 years running from love. I would get into relationships with inappropriate men always in fear of falling in love and getting hurt. Past experiences would get in the way of me making balanced healthy decisions. Instead I would replay the situation from 8th grade where my first boyfriend cheated on me, and then called me a fat slut on the school bus. Ever since then, I had been replaying this same story in my mind. I kept picking men who would belittle my place in the world by making comments about my weight, and I continued to not trust men. The little voice in our heads has a funny way of making the past a reality. By replaying the story, I was able to stay in a state of constant denial. I was denying my true self. I was running from love because my only experience of romantic love was a boy who called me a fat slut.

After I got my dog, Tucker, I learned what real love is. He helped open my heart to receive and give unconditional love. I realized that the feelings I share with my dog are real love, because real love does not hurt. Real love does not judge or make fun of anyone. Real love is kind, compassionate, expansive, and forgiving. Real love is unconditional and never ends. **I will repeat that real love is unconditional and never ends.** We all come from love. We are born into this world filled up with love as it pours out of our little chubby, hairless bodies. Then something happens that makes us question love. Our parents fight, we get into trouble, other people make fun of us. Whatever it is we think, "This isn't right. If this is love I don't want to be part of it." So we build up these little walls that eventually become giant walls that are almost impossible to crash down.

I know because I lived through this. I was Miss Independent, don't come near me. I had the reputation of being a man-eater. I would keep men at a distance, all in an attempt to protect myself and keep them from calling me fat or slutty. I fought through eating disorders and depression in an attempt to protect myself from the "evil doings" of love. My soul would cry out, I would come home from sexcapades or bathroom bulimic sessions and come crashing to the floor. My soul would say, "This is not right, my dear friend." I craved love, I needed to give love, and I had so much love to give this world, but I was denying myself this natural pleasure. I wasn't alone. Think of your life, and see if you have been running from love. Maybe it is the relationship with you. I was a victim of self-abuse. Whether it was sex, drugs or food I was unloving to myself. But we are all beings of love and it is our right and purpose to love and be loved.

Making a connection with other people is one of the most magical things we can do to brighten our day and theirs. Smile at a stranger. Help a blind person cross the street. Buy the coffee of the person standing behind you. Do small acts of kindness that show generous nuggets of love. When you do this you will see a shift in your outer world. I started to do all of this, and it works, trust me.

In a Nutshell:

1. Accept what is to get to what you want.
2. Focus on what you want, not on what you have.
3. Smile more.
4. Everyone just wants to be loved.

Additional Resources:

Audio Meditation: *Find Your Happy: Motivational Mantras*, Track 7, "Perfect Just the Way You Are" (available on iTunes, <u>amazon.com</u>, and <u>playwiththeworld.com</u> shop).

CHAPTER SIX

MONEY IS YOUR FRIEND

"Don't judge each day by the harvest you reap
but by the seeds you plant." — *Robert Louis Stevenson*

Money is a touchy subject because people either love it or hate it. People seem to either have a lot of it, or not enough. Money issues cause fights, anger, and even divorce. People use money for power, attention, to mask insecurities, to feel better, and more. I ask people what they want more than anything else in the world. After they answer, I ask, "Why don't you have it?" Most of the time the answer I hear is, "I don't have enough money," or "It costs too much money," followed by a close second excuse, "I don't have enough time." Time and money are similar because they both put limitations on our dreams if we let them. It takes an ability to release our attachment to what money can and can't do for us in order to break through to live our ultimate life. Let's look at money and how it relates to our dreams.

Money Doesn't Buy Security

When I ask people why they want more money, the rallying cry is always to feel more secure and be able to do the things they want to do. But, in general, people who make more money are often less happy than those who make less. When people make more money they tend to spend more money, often leaving a larger deficit in their bank accounts. I know this from personal experience. When I was working in Chicago, I was making almost $70,000 a year. When I returned to Oregon, in my transition, I took a job that paid $10 an hour and for the most part I was happier and more satisfied with my life because I was doing what I loved, writing. I was surrounded by like-minded people and living on the West Coast. How can someone go from making almost six figures to just over minimum wage in less than a month and manage to find peace? For me it was about letting go of expectations. My expectations for my life and what I thought I should be doing at specific ages and how much I thought I should be making needed to subside. **The truth is we are always going to have enough money for what we need.**

When I was in Chicago, I lived in a giant loft three blocks from the Sears Tower. I had a larger-than-life lifestyle that needed a large salary to support it. Once I shifted and realized my depression was attached to my current lifestyle, my needs changed. I no longer needed a big loft in a big city, working at a big advertising agency. All of it seemed so forced and unnatural to me. As soon as I realized this, my outside world shifted to match my internal state because I was laid off. Suddenly, my lifestyle could not be supported by the drastic shift in my income level. The lifestyle no longer served my higher good and me, so the large income disappeared simply to show me a more acceptable way to live my life. Moving from making $70,000 a year to being unemployed can do some damage to the ego, but I used this opportunity to propel me into my future dream self. I knew that advertising and its fancy green dollars no longer helped me fulfill my mission in life. The money became secondary and was no longer a driving force in my life. Once I moved to Portland, I happily took a job for $10 an hour. I noticed all of my bills were still paid, and I had even more money, because I was making an effort to save. By not having such high overhead, I could afford to make smarter choices and have a lower income to support my new outlook on life. It is not about money. With such a drastic shift, I learned money did not buy me security.

Money does have a funny way of driving our decisions in life. Often the more money we make, the more we spend. In order to feel like you have more money, look at where you are spending your money and ask if that serves your highest intention. For example, if one of your dreams is to take a cruise with your sweetheart but you spend over $25 a day on Starbucks and eating out, ask yourself, "Is this what I really want?" Your daily habits could add up to nearly $700 a month that could go towards your dream vacation. **Our choices make the biggest difference in how we relate to money.**

Perhaps you have said, "If only I could win the lottery." Well, winning millions of dollars may still not provide security. Many lottery winners would say, "Be careful what you wish for." We have all heard the urban myths about people winning the lottery and losing it all. Luke Pittard won 1.9 million the UK lottery. A year and a half later he had blown through the money and was forced to take a job at McDonalds. Any quick Google search of lottery winners' stories will bring up pages of people who had it all and lost it to drugs, alcohol, handouts, and other poor choices. This simply proves that more money does not always provide more security, and may potentially lead to greater insecurity.

Money Is Energy

My challenge was to let go of the mindset that money could provide anything more than a means of exchanging one good for another. When we take a step back and look at money for what it really is, we can release all emotional attachments. Money in itself brings up a lot of things for many people, but if we learn to look at it as energy and a simple form of payment for one good or service in exchange for another, then we can lessen its burden on our emotional state. By focusing our attention on what we want and spending our time doing what we love, we will attract money to ourselves.

When we are in a state of lack or fearful thought patterns money cannot come to us because we are in a needy state, and when we need something the experience is strained. Think about a situation in your life when a person needed your help. There are different types of needs. Sometimes people ask others for help because they are at a crossroads or need some guidance on how to proceed forward. Naturally, they may reach out to their support system to ask for help, and it will be easy for people to help them. When the help needed involves desperate demands, it is harder to help.

Recently, my friend asked if I could help her plan some wedding stuff. She spent nine months procrastinating and not listening to anyone's advice or guidance to help her plan an awesome wedding. Every time I had asked her how I could help, she would blow it off and ignore the offer. Four weeks away from the wedding, she finally began to have an "Oh crap" moment and began making rather demanding requests of everyone who wanted to be there for her earlier. Because her energy was desperate and stressed out, it was hard for me to give her the help she needed.

The same energy that occurs in relationships happens with the exchange of money. If you are in a desperate state of needing money because you feel the lack, money cannot come to you. You cannot be abundant if you feel poor. However you can be poor and feel abundant. It is a matter of perception and shifting your mind to focus on what you want. How much money do you need to do the things you want to do? How much money do you want to save? Asking and answering key questions will allow your mind to expand and move out of a state of depression.

When money flows to us, it is important to accept it and let it flow through us, which means letting it leave us just as comfortably. One way to know what your energy is towards money is to ask yourself if you are comfortable spending money. If you answered no, then you are like I used to be. I had to learn that money would always flow and come and go. People who worry about spending money or freeze up and stress out when it is time to whip out the money for the bill fall into a category I like to call the "lack lusters." The fear of lack takes over and stirs their thoughts to worry about the future. Esther and Jerry Hicks teach from the Abrahams and described this experience in the book, *Money and the Law of Attraction*. The authors suggest, "When you believe that money is coming to you because of your action that you are offering and you also believe that you will not always be able to offer that action, you would want to hold on to your money and spend it sparingly to make it last. However the feeling of shortage slows down the process of money flowing to you." If you are feeling uncomfortable while spending money, do not spend money. Always find a way to ease your discomfort and transform each transition into a peaceful experience. Understanding that money flows and goes is one thing that helped me.

Money Flows and Goes

We do not focus on taking in all of the breath we need for the entire year to survive, but rather breathe constantly in and out. We can look at money the same way. By releasing our energetic hold on money it loosens its superficial power. Just like breathing in and out easily, money can flow in and out of our experience with the same gentle ease as life itself.

This is the ultimate goal of success and feeling abundant: to allow money to enter in and exit with ease and no expectations. From personal experience I know that money flows in and disappears within seconds. Remember, I was making over $2,500 a week with what I thought was comfortable job security, but all of it disappeared.

When we attach the amount of money we make to our own importance we will always fall off the throne. I had convinced myself that I was a big shot because I could afford all the social luxuries. I was using money to define my own identity. I made X amount, but I wouldn't be happy until I made X amount. I could never figure out that money doesn't want to control us or lead us into the path of temptation. The little voices in our heads make money the hero in our lives, but money is not a superhero. It will not solve all of the world's problems or fix what is broken inside of us.

Many people use retail therapy as a form of masking and covering up the holes in their hearts. Not wanting to look at our emotions or feel them, we shop over them, spend money over them, and maybe even lose all of our money over them. Money cannot buy happiness. The only thing that can is love. The love we try to buy with money is always temporary and fleeting. Money can't buy love, but we believe the pretty new clothes, the makeup and fancy dresses, cars and homes will make us happier. So we whip out the credit card to pay for what we can't purchase now. According to www.mutualimprovement.com, the average American household is $15,000 in credit card debt. With interest, that will take over 25 years to pay off or 40 years if you are just paying the bare minimum. Imagine a life without debt, loans, or paybacks. What if your world was debt free? What would you be able to do with your time, money, and energy if you weren't focused on paying off larger debts? That is one of the points of *Find Your Happy*. In order to live a happy, free and fulfilled life, we need to free ourselves of what confines us.

If you have bills that seem overwhelming, there are certain steps you can take to make yourself feel free on the journey to pay them back. Instead of focusing on all of the money you owe and the things you can't buy because you have to make payments, focus on what you want. For the past few years one of my big goals has been to travel to Brazil, so I started to create a mental field trip on manifesting this Brazil trip. A mental field trip focuses on what you want, sets up an intention and describes why you want it. Then you take action steps towards it. The universe will respond to your desires if they are aligned to your higher good.

The specific trip I want to take will be $3,500-$4,500, and I just didn't know where that money would come from. But I continued to focus on what I wanted and did not let the fact that I did not have the money stop me. I sent in a deposit on the trip to move my goal into action. By taking steps toward your goal you will show the universe you are serious and things can align to help you reach your dream. For me, after I sent in my deposit for the trip, things started to flow. All of a sudden more coaching clients were coming to me, along with more design and publishing clients, and my business started to double in revenue. Less then two months later I had mad enough to pay for my trip to see Jon of God, a healer in Brazil. I share this story to demonstrate the power of intention. I did not let the fact that I "did not have" enough money stop me from pursuing my dream. Look at your own life and see where you are using "not enough money" as an excuse. You can recognize it as an excuse and take action, despite of the fact, and move towards your dream. It worked for me, I know it will work for you.

Spending Money Is Just as Important as Saving It

When I was making a lot of money, I didn't focus on saving it. It wasn't until I started to make less money that I found a balance between saving and earning. I remember my sophomore economics teacher telling us that if we saved 10% of every paycheck from the moment we turned 18, we would retire multimillionaires. That notion of saving 10% stayed in the back of my mind whether I actually saved or not. There is a balance of money-in and money-out. Sometimes people have subconscious fears concerning spending money. Remember when we discussed the difference between people who don't feel comfortable spending money vs. those that spend with ease? The people who are uncomfortable with spending money may have a deeper underlying fear that there is never enough to go around. By worrying about a lack of money, these fears can manifest into either saving all of their money and being fearful of where to spend it, or spending it all and feeling ashamed for having nothing in the bank and bouncing yet another check. There is no difference between saving and spending money if your energetic state is in fear of losing it all. People who worry that there is not enough to go around cannot receive more money or allow abundance to flow until they learn to accept that the universe is plentiful and generous with its gifts. I know this from personal experience; I have been on both sides of the spectrum. I worried that money would disappear and then it did disappear and I had no idea where my next paycheck would be coming from.

This is why focusing on saving 10% of everything you make will help you feel more comfortable in unplanned situations. If you have a little bit of savings you feel empowered and more secure with the ability to make choices. You could use that money for that vacation to Belize, for French lessons, or just keep it to spend on a pack of bubble gum. It doesn't really matter what you spend it on if you spend it for you. You save it for yourself and treat yourself. Don't give it all away, or spend it on every other person but youself. You are the most important person in your world. If you are not cared for, loved and treated with kindness by you, yourself, then no one else can do that for you.

Spending money is just as important as saving it. Sometimes people worry about job security and where their money will come from, so they tend to hoard all of their money. They don't spend it and this creates the same energetic static that happens with people who are worried about spending all their funds, and then lose it all because they go out on a shop-a-thon. Spending money on things you really care about is the goal with exchanging money. If you really want to go skydiving but tell yourself it is too much money, while every day you are spending money on parking meters, coffee and gas for your car, then maybe there is a better way to get what you want. If the things you are spending your money on don't align with what you want out of your life then you can change the outcome. Simply switch your spending habits. The first step is to look at your habits to see if you need a shift.

Awesome Opportunity:

1. What is something you really want but don't have yet because you keep saying you don't have enough money? It could be something material, or an experience.
2. Each day, what do you spend most of your money on right now?
3. How much money per month do you spend on disposable things? Pull out a bank statement and look at where your money is going. Separate your expenses into three categories: bills, disposable (coffee, meals out, new clothes material goods, manicure, social life, etc.) and dreams.
Bills _____
Disposable _____
Dreams _____

The dream category is the fun category that includes your hopes, goals, money towards learning something new, a cooking class, or language lessons. Money in this category is for things on your list of things to do in your life. These are experiences; therefore they are investments in your life.

Now that I am a writer, I love working from coffee shops. But when I realized that I was spending over $40 a week at Starbucks, light bulbs went off like flickering spotlights. If I just cut back, I could save over $1,000 in six months. *Voilà!* There is my plane ticket to Brazil! The money-in, money-out balance is all about focusing on priorities and making sure your needs are met. By no means am I a money expert. We have people like Suze Orman for that. But I do have a hefty list of things I am tackling before I exit planet earth, and the reality is that all of them require money. So how do we make the money to spend on the things we love?

Making Money Has Nothing To Do with Your Job

For the longest time, I believed that the money I made was only connected to the job I performed. In the technical sense, yes, of course it was, but in the energetic sense it was not. Stay with me for a moment. I spent many years suffering in a job that denied me joy, but the money was so fantastic I convinced myself that everyone needed to pretend to be happy so we can get the paycheck, pay our bills, and feel guilty for requesting vacation time off. We tie money to the jobs we take. One common thing we think is the only way to get security with steady money is through "The Man," corporate America. It took me many years of pushing and pulling with my internal self to realize that the job I take doesn't have to be my career. Just like mini chapters of a book, jobs are chapters in our working life. The real career is life.

As soon as I let go of the expectation of taking a job because of a steady paycheck, I felt more secure than ever before. I recognized that money would always come and go. In learning that our career does not define us or make us who we are, we let go of the demands we put on the dollar bill. The notion of making our lives our career is far more interesting to me. If we think about what a career can do for us in the traditional sense, we can break apart the elements and apply it to our lives.

A career is designed to provide a platform for professional growth. It is a place to feel a sense of worth and contribution. Careers help people define what they want. The days of staying in one career for an entire lifetime died when the baby boomers were born. With so many fantastic opportunities and so many precious people wanting to reach their full potential, it's almost mandatory for us to explore. Humans, by nature, are curious creatures and we want to see what is available to us. Finding a perfect career takes time.

Too often, people settle into a comfortable existence where they skate through on just enough effort to make sure they keep getting that paycheck. They zombie home to watch negative news and play video games, only to wake up more lethargic than the day before. This book isn't for them; you are reading this book because you want more out of your life. Whether you are looking for a career shift, or wanting to feel freer in your everyday life, choosing to accept your life in the present moment is the key to abundance.

Nothing is forever. The job you are in, the boss you have, the amount of money you make is all temporary, a moment in time in your present story. As your story unfolds you grow, change, need more, want less, etc. The point is the amount of money you make right now and the job you are doing right now, is not your permanent state. We put so much pressure on ourselves, and cause even more stress, by assuming that our lives are not the way we planned. The problem with trying to be somewhere you are not is you are not accepting or appreciating where you are. By simply shifting our perception to appreciate the moment we have, we can loosen our tension with money and our jobs.

Give without Expecting

It's been said that there are two types of people: those who give freely and those who give expecting something in return. It is possible to cross over into both categories, but generally there is one you can relate to most. Being more generous echoes the golden rule: Do unto others as you wish them to do unto you. Giving without expecting anything in return will open you up to new opportunities. There is a balance of energy that exists when you freely give yourself, your time, your energy, or your money to someone or something you believe in. Ask yourself how you can serve someone else.

I learned about this concept through my mentor relationship with best-selling author, spiritual guru Gabrielle Bernstein. She and I were connected in the beginning through a mishap when I ordered some books from her online store. She had gifted me one free coaching session for a delay in the book order. As we were talking on the phone, she discovered that I was a graphic designer while she happened to be looking for a new designer that very week. Soon, I became her full-time designer, and she was my full-time, spiritual running buddy and writing coach. The fact that she gave her time to me for a free coaching session and was not expecting anything back allowed both of us to be open to the beautiful friendship we now have.

When I talk about giving without expecting anything in return, I am not just talking about money. Sometimes we don't have money to give, but we have time and energy. If we spend all of our lives running the line, "I have no time, or energy, or money," then we are not even giving to ourselves. Why are we filling up our schedules with so much stuff? *Find Your Happy* is meant to help us remove this extraneous stuff so we can be free and light on our feet. It starts with giving and forgiving. We already talked about forgiving so here we are looking at giving. Bottom line is the more you give the more you will receive. The universe will gift you in more abundance when you share your gifts, talents, energy, time, and money.

Awesome Opportunity:

1. What have you not given yourself that you know you want? (More time for yourself, a special gift you've been eyeballing for months, a trip?)
2. What is the reason you have not allowed yourself to get what you want?
3. Now flip the coin and look at what you are not giving to other people. (Time, attention, listening?)
4. Where do you think you can give a little more to both your personal life and others?
5. What do you think would happen if you gave to other people what they are not currently getting?
6. For the next week, practice giving. Start to say yes to life and give yourself fully to life in every possible way.

In a Nutshell:

1. We are always going to have enough money for what we need. The universe always has us covered and the universe never gives us more than we can handle.
2. Our choices make the biggest difference in how we relate to money. We get what we give.
3. Money should not be tied to a career. Your life is your career and money will always support your life.
4. The universe will gift you in more abundance when you share your gifts, talents, energy, time, and money.
5. Spending money is just as important as saving it.

Additional Resources:

Audio Meditation: *Find Your Happy: Motivational Mantras*, Track 12, "Be Thankful" (available on iTunes, amazon.com, and playwiththeworld.com shop).

CHAPTER SEVEN

BECOME A MASTER MANIFESTER. SET GOALS.

"Success means having the courage, the determination, and the will to become the person you believe you were meant to be." — *George Sheehan*

Focus on What You Want

The power in setting goals is tremendous. The wealthiest people in the world set goals. A goal is simply a vision or dream realized. The dictionary defines it as the destination of a journey, but I believe the journey is part of a goal. It is just as important to work towards a desired outcome as it is to achieve that outcome. People who make goals are not always go-getters, entrepreneurs, or self-motivated people. These are all certainly helpful traits to have, but anyone can make goals. Anyone can achieve outstanding success from having a clearly defined focus.

I make three-month goals, six-month goals, and one-year goals. I also make weekly goals, and my results are profound. When I write something down, it is amazing how the brain goes to work at solving the hows, and busts through obstacles. Sometimes I make a goal for six months out and in one month I realize it has been reached. That is the power of creating a magnificent life. Setting goals is the cornerstone to designing a spectacular you. The first step is to focus on what you want.

We all have situations in our lives that might not be working as well as we would like, but focusing on the things that aren't working will not get us any closer to achieving a goal. Say you want a new car because your current car is breaking down all the time. If you focus your energy on the fact that your car is unreliable, your energy will be exhausted on the problem, not on the solution. If you shift your energy and mindset to focus on what you want, a new Jeep Wrangler, let's say, you will find this goal will be realized faster than if you did not think about it. Do you ever notice when you start thinking about things, they suddenly appear in your world? This is not an accident, whether it is a type of car, a dog or even the name of a person. When we focus our energy on things we want, we will always manifest them to reality. If you want to lose weight, focus on the feelings of being lighter, your clothes fitting better, and the world responding to the new, thin, vibrant you. It will be impossible to lose weight if you are currently in a state of self-hate, pity, and overindulgence. If you look in the mirror and ridicule yourself for being pudgy, then your goal of losing weight becomes much harder to achieve. Making goals is the first part. Feeling your goals is the key that people often skip over.

Feeling Your Goals and the Power of Vision Boards

It is important to be clear about what you want, but that is only the first part to making your dreams a reality. There are six main aspects to reaching your goals.

1. Be clear – make a desire statement.
2. Focus on what you want.
3. Act towards it.
4. State the intention of your goal.
5. Let go of the how.
6. Keep focusing on what you want until it happens.

As I said earlier, being clear is often the hardest part. **Many people don't know what they want so they keep getting what they don't want.** When you align yourself with a clear focus, you have a direction to work towards, a blueprint to set you on the right path to making your dreams a reality. I make desire statements and then I say them every day. To help manifest what you want, you can make desire statements too.

How to make a desire statement:

1. Think about what you want and write it down in one sentence or less. (I want to own a new car, for example.)
2. Now be as specific as possible and make it present tense. Rather than "I want," or "I will," say "I own," etc. and put a date to which you want to accomplish your goal. ("I own a red Jeep Wrangler soft-top by July 30.")
3. Now that you have a desire statement you can repeat this every day (or why not every hour?) to help you stay focused.

I continue to update, change and revise my desire statements but the beauty is that with each new statement I have more focus. These statements can help you not only manifest more quickly but also help you see the power of intention in action.

The second part to making goals a reality is to focus on what you want. It will help you get to what you want much faster than wasting energy on what you don't want. Think about something you wanted in the past and actually got. Most likely you were thinking about it a lot. Perhaps you started to see it more, and most likely without much effort you got it. That is the beauty of thinking positively and focusing on the good things. You will get more good things, and rather quickly.

The third part to making goals a reality is to act towards it. I have a goal to be a best-selling book author, so every day I am working on my platform, developing larger networks and updating my website. Every day, take at least one action towards your goal, whether it is a phone call, research online, or buying a book to learn more about it. Taking a step towards what you want not only shows the universe you are serious, but it puts you in line for opportunities to come your way. In my workshops and lectures, I tell people to do one thing everyday that you future-self will thank you for.

The fourth part many people skip over because it seems rather obvious. Ask yourself, "Why do I want this?" Most of us say because it will make us happy to get it, but I challenge you to dig a little deeper and find the root of the goal. If you want to lose weight, you may think it will make you happier but what is the deeper reason? Maybe the reason is because you want to love and accept yourself more or you want to live longer and be healthier. I want to be a best-selling book author so my message can get out to the masses, rather than the few. The more people I can serve the more fulfilled I am because I want to make a difference in other peoples' lives. Where as the surface aspect of my goal might be, I want to be a best selling author to establish my writing career. Only until I dug deeper could I reveal the real reasons. Ask yourself, "Why do I want this?" Many times we can learn more about ourselves by seeing the root of the goal.

The fifth and hardest part about setting and manifesting goals is to let go of the how. When we want something, we usually set out a clear path about how we are going to get it. This can sometimes set up a blockade to prevent us from getting what we really want. We try to figure out who we need to call, how we need to accomplish the goal, but nine times out of ten the goal is realized in ways we never thought possible.

For example, say you want a new car and you go to the bank to get a loan. The bank denies you, and instead of refocusing your goal, you give up because the "how" in your mind wasn't met. You thought getting a loan from the bank was "how" you would reach your goal, but when that "how" didn't fall into place, your expectations were shattered.

It is hard, but learning to let go of the how and trust that your goal WILL happen is part of reaching your goals. If you continue to focus on the new car and how it will make you feel, then the bank denying you will be nothing more than little bump in the day. No worries, there will be a better way. Let's say you go to the dealership and they approve you on the spot and give you $3,000 off because of a weekend special. This same scenario happened to me when I bought my dream car, my Jeep Wrangler.

I wouldn't have received that offer through a bank loan. The moral of the story is, if you give up on your dream because the "how" doesn't match up to how you thought your goal would be realized then you may not reach your goal. Let go to let your goals come true. The universe always has a plan greater than ours.

The sixth and final part of reaching your goal is to keep focusing on it until it happens. Ninety-five percent of people give up before actually reaching their goal. What about the other five percent? What do they do that makes their luminous dreams come true? They don't give up. It is as simple as that. Many people believe that focusing on what you want is a good way to start, but after time goes by and they haven't received what they want in the physical form, they give up and say this "manifesting focus mumbo jumbo doesn't work." Then they shift their thoughts to what doesn't work in their lives, and the negative things that are happening. If they held the thoughts of what they wanted, and continued to say the desire statement out loud every day they will always get what they want. By giving up, the channel to receive what they want is closed down. It can no longer come to you if you are not willing to receive it. I believe this is the hardest, but most important, part of making goals come true: stay clear and focused until you are successful. It doesn't matter if it takes a week, a year, or five years. Keep focusing on what you want because it is on its way to you.

Create a Magic List

Welcome, friends, to one of the best parts of your *Love Your Life to the Fullest* journey. Creating a magic list is as simple as asking, "What experiences of a lifetime do I want to enjoy?" We get to map out what we want, and this is the best tool to access the unlimited potential of being fulfilled at every moment in our lives.

When I was 14, I sat down and wrote on the top of a legal pad, "List of Things to Do Before I Die," and I started to write. Within 15 minutes, I had already filled up three pages with places, experiences, and things to do. I didn't realize I had so many dreams tucked inside because this was the first opportunity I gave myself to let them out. Finally, the things I held dearest to my heart had a platform to breathe, to grow, and to live.

A magic list is simply a list of things to do during your life. I don't like calling it a bucket list because that focuses on kicking the can versus the actual awesomeness wrapped up in each experience. I like to call it a magic list, which I find more fitting since it allows you to unleash the fascination, charm, and glamour that come with creating a powerful life. The list becomes a source of inspiration when you need a little boost. Once created, the magic list also becomes an indicator of what you value most in your life by highlighting the key things you want to experience.

When I think back over the years since I created that original list, the things that stand out most in my mind are the highlights of the special experiences that were on my list like swimming with wild dolphins, owning a Jeep Wrangler, adopting a golden retriever, skydiving, bungee jumping, hang-gliding, cooking well, and the list goes on. All of these experiences conjure up romantic moments of intimate self-expression. When we make a list and work towards checking things off, we show ourselves that we matter. We put time aside to make ourselves feel loved and cared for. Your inner child will thank you, and so will everyone else around you because when you are happy and smiling because you are doing what you love, the rest of the world will smile along with you.

Why make a list of things to do during your life?

Similar to setting goals, making a list can give you focus and infinite amounts of clarity about what you want to achieve in life. If you don't have a list, but say things like, "Oh it would be fun to skydive, but I could never afford it," or "I've always wanted to be a better cook, but I don't have the time," chances are these are just "wouldn't it be nice" ideas. I know this merry-go-around very well because I played the game for most of my life until I refocused on what I really wanted and recognized that **happiness must start from within.** When we turn to our special magic list we become focused and excited. When we are excited about things, we are passionate and full of energy. Time, money and energy seem plentiful because when we are inspired, time is infinite and so are the resources related to how and when to achieve our goals.

The list of things to do during your life is the single most important tool to accessing your potential. It is your dream list, so why wouldn't you want to make one? Life moves pretty fast and it is up to us to make every second count. The whole point of the magic list is to maximize every moment of our existence and live our lives to the fullest. It's a reminder of all the things we want to achieve in our awesome, fun-filled life so that instead of wasting time in pointless activities and being bored and tired, we are directing our energy fully toward what matters most to us. Are you ready to create an awesome power-punched list? Let's start by answering some key questions.

1. If you won the lottery and had an unlimited amount of money what would you do with your day?
2. If you were to die tonight what regrets would you have?
3. What is one place you have always wanted to go?
4. What is something you have always wanted to learn?
5. What achievements would you like to accomplish by next year?
6. What have you always wanted to do, but have not done yet?
7. What are your biggest goals and dreams?
8. Five years from now, where do you want to be in your life?
9. Close your eyes. What is the first thing that comes to your mind? Put it on your magic list.

The best part about making this list is that it is all about you so, technically, it shouldn't be too hard. All you need to do is check in with yourself, ask what you want, and then let your mind go. It doesn't matter how big or silly a goal may be. The list is for you and your life; no one else needs to put his or her two cents in. If you want to break the Guinness World Record for baking the largest vegan chocolate chip cookie, then go for it. Don't let the non-vegans stop you. You know what is best for you, and you must always follow that instinct. If your significant other, or family, or boss doesn't understand, that doesn't matter for you. We cannot live our lives trying to please the rest of the world because then we end up making everyone semi-satisfied as we sacrifice our own happiness. I am not saying ignore all laws and disrespect those you love, but simply find a balance between what matters most to you in life and move towards that with everything you have.

As you treat your magic list like a free write, make sure to leave the excuses, justifications, and negative posses at the door. They are not welcome here, so kick them out. The only thing you need to focus on is your hopes, wishes, and dreams. Do not be concerned with how goals are going to come true, but focus on the feelings that you'll get when you accomplish them. What will it feel like when you cook an entire Thanksgiving meal by yourself or when you become a best-selling published author? Put those dreams down, and don't be creating excuses about why they aren't going to happen. The only rule to the magic list is to ask what you want. You do not need to solve the problem of how it will happen, so relax a bit and enjoy the process.

Now that you have an awesome blossom list of things to do, share it with people you love. We all have a go-to person or group who is supportive of our dreams. Share your top three with them and watch their eyes light up. When we share with other people, they get excited in the process, too. Plus, enrolling others and sharing your goals makes them more of a reality because you have others to follow-up and hold you accountable. People aren't there to slap your hand if you don't go skydiving this month because it is on your list, but they will support you when you do go. When you share yourself with people, they will naturally feel closer to you.

Blueprint Your Life

One of the coolest things about the magic list of things to do during your life is that it sets out a framework for your life. It provides a blueprint for you to do everything you want and more. Imagine being on your deathbed and having no regrets, no incompletes, no karmic drama, just peace, love, and complete fulfillment. That is what this list will do for you. After looking over your first goals, you may see a pattern. Things that are most important to you will rise to the top. You will immediately begin to see what you value most in life. Places you want to go, experiences you want to have, and people you want to meet will all be ready to assist you because you have created a clear intention that you want do these things too. You can set aside special dates to accomplish specific goals. Once you have laid out a grand list you can start circling the ones you want to check off sooner rather than later. You can look at the ones that seem far off and put a date by them. The blueprint for your life sets up a type of corporate you. You are the CEO of you and you get to call the shots. So what will you be doing this month? Skydiving? Cooking class? Reading a book you never read? Dig into life and let your magic list flow.

Vision Boards

All of this magic talk and focusing on what you want is great, but it is missing part of its program. In order to be a superstar manifester, focusing on what you want will yield the best results if you use visualization. One of the best ways to do that is to create a vision board illustrating your goals. It can contain pictures, quotes, things cut out of magazines, anything that inspires you. It doesn't have to be a concrete image of the specific things you want but simply an inspiring image. The goal is for the vision board to evoke feelings of happiness and fulfillment. For example, things on my vision board are, "Live life to the fullest," a picture of an elephant trekking in Thailand, a red Jeep Wrangler, and a lottery ticket with the handwritten word: "WINNER." The vision board is a fun way to let your imagination play. Making the most out of life is simply enjoying every second, and when we create vision boards we can enjoy the process of letting our hearts go wild. So what is it that you want? What things inspire you? Maybe there is a person you admire. Go to his or her website and get their photo to put on your board. Maybe you want to go to Africa. Post a picture of Africa on your board or a plane ticket to Africa or even a symbol that represents Africa to you. Have fun making your dreams come to life in your vision board and let your imagination go. The beautiful part about making a vision board is it puts our hopes and dreams into pictures and sayings on an actual board we can see daily. I put my board on my office door, so every time I sit at my desk, I see the board. I have to update my vision board often because goals come true rather quickly. When you do all of the steps laid out in this section you, too, will become a master manifester in lickety split time.

Awesome Opportunity:

1. For the next 21 days, focus on something you really want.
2. Make a desire statement and read it every morning when you get up.
3. Spend at least five minutes every day picturing you doing your desire statement.

In a Nutshell:

1. Focus on what you want, not what you don't want, to get more of what you want.
2. Practice feeling your goals to make them a reality.
3. The best tool to creating a fulfilling life is creating a list of things you want to do during your lifetime.
4. Creating a vision board will help you manifest faster.

Additional Resources:

Audio Meditation: *Find Your Happy: Motivational Mantras,* Track 5, "Focus on What You Want" (available on iTunes, amazon.com, and playwiththeworld.com shop).

CHAPTER EIGHT

BECOME A "YES!" PERSON

"It is not uncommon for people to spend their whole life waiting to start living." — *Eckhart Tolle*

This is my favorite chapter because if you choose to take in what I share here, you will see gigantic, transformative results in your life. Things you cannot even imagine at this moment will become available to you. Just by saying, "Yes!" to life, opportunities will reveal themselves to you in ways that leave you floored, amazed, and in awe.

In 2008, Jim Carrey stared in a movie called *Yes Man*. A shy, reserved man named Carl is at a standstill in life until the day he enrolls in a personal development program based on the very simple idea to say "Yes!" to everything. Carl discovers with amazement the magical power of "Yes!" and sees his professional and romantic life turned upside down overnight when he receives an unexpected promotion and meets a new girlfriend.

After I watched the movie I thought there might be something to this "Yes!" thing. At the time, I was in a place of regimented routine. I would wake up in the morning, work out, go to work, come home and say no to social opportunities because I was so depressed. I was unhappy and just numbed the pain by working long hours, working out extra long or plopping in front of the TV to escape from the nothingness I was getting stale in. I related to the character in the movie because I felt like I was at a standstill and had nothing to look forward to. That changed, of course, when the New Year came around and I decided to issue a New Year's "Resolution" Challenge. For two weeks I had to say, "Yes!"

to everything. If the little voice in my head signaled "No!" I would go against it and say, "Yes!" For two weeks only I would became a "Yes!" person. What happened soon after is miraculous. When the little voice in my head, the voice of comfort said, "Whoa, lady, you are in uncharted territory," that is right where I lived for two weeks.

Chuck Excuses to the Curb

If there is something you want to do but have reasons for not doing it, these are excuses. I call excuses the things we tell ourselves to justify staying in our comfort zones. They range from, "I don't have enough time," to "I am too tired." Often excuses hide out in what a lot of people like to call "reality."

In my private coaching sessions and workshops, I often meet people who hold on to a lot of excuses. I work with them to remove these barriers that keep them from getting what they want. I recently coached a guy named "Vinnie." He is a man who has a daughter and a family to feed. He is working in a sales position at a giant industrial corporation. He knows that he is underpaid and overworked, but he doesn't complain. He doesn't stick his head out or take any risks. He does what he is told and stays comfortable knowing that he has a paycheck coming every two weeks.

I asked Vinnie what he wanted to be when he was a child. He explained that he would always race around, protecting his make-believe friends and making sure justice was served. He wanted to be a police officer, a man of righteous duty. Now he is an adult and that daydream is just a fleeting thought. However, every time he hears a police siren race by, a glimmer of that dream comes back. His dream is to be a police officer, even as a 34-year-old man.

Dreams never die. Sometimes they change form and morph into bigger granddaddy dreams but the essence of what we want stays the same. Another thing about dreams is they are patient. Dreams are quiet and accommodating. They put themselves on the back burner while you are "realistic," while you are "responsible" and while you ignore them. Dreams don't ask anything from you, except for the possibility of entertaining them.

I asked Vinnie, "Why aren't you a police officer?" he respond, "Because I have a little girl and a family to feed. I need to be responsible and take care of her," as if following his heart would be somehow irresponsible. Does this sound familiar to you? The reality is, all of us have a little Vinnie in us. Vinnie is practical, responsible and conscientious. He is anything but unstable; his middle name is playing it safe, whereas the dreamers in all of us are anything but safe. Dreamers are wild, spontaneous, and overflowing with exuberance and joy. Yet, the dreamers are not full of excuses. They are full of feeling and doing. That is the difference between "doing the right thing" and "doing what feels right." By doing the right thing, the responsible adult in us doesn't rock the boat, is mentally safe, and full of excuses. But when did playing it safe ever make us happy? And furthermore, when you hide your true self from the world, you are not doing the right thing for you or the people closest to you. Most of us walk around in a shell of a human in fear of losing our jobs. Fear feeds us from the moment we wake up, and we lose sight of what we really want. Our minds stomp on our dreams and tell us that they will never happen. **We play it safe for fear of losing what we have.**

What would happen if we pushed through that fear? Andre Gide said, "Man cannot discover new oceans unless he has the courage to lose sight of the shore." If we are too afraid to push out of our comfort zone then we can never grow. We will never be able to see the other side. Our job in life is to be happy, and being happy means taking risks. It means chucking excuses to the curb and trusting the universe will and can provide for all of our dreams. There is no shortage of resources to go around. The most beautiful part about having goals is that they are yours personally. No one else has the same dream. I said it before, but this quote is valuable. Oprah said, **"You are here to do something uniquely created for you. No one else can do it like you can. That is why you are here."**

No matter what your dream is, only you can do it the way you can, so push through your comfort zone and see what is on the other side. **We all have a series of great opportunities that are disguised as impossible situations.** It is those situations that help us grow and feel life to its fullest.

In my coaching with Vinnie, I recognized his dedication to be a family provider. I asked him "What type of life would you be leading if you did follow your heart?" He realized that if he chose to pursue his dream as a police officer and left his corporate job to be what he wants in his heart, his daughter would see that anything is possible in life, that she really can be anything and everything she wants to be because her hero, her father, is pursuing his dream. He would be setting a good example for his child, showing her to never settle. He would inevitably gain more respect from his current coworkers who are stuck in the same comfort zone as well. When he leaves the company to announce he is pursuing his dream to be a police officer, looks of amazement and awe will follow him. People will be inspired by him and respect the courage he has shown, but most important is Vinnie and his personal relationship with himself. By putting his dreams into focus he is able to love himself fully. He is saying to the world, "I am worth it and my dreams matter." When he pursues his dream, the stars seem to align, and he even earns more money doing what he loves.

Vinnie's life is no longer about mundane ritual and comfortable responsibilities. He lives from a place of love for himself and respect for his life. He understands that his actions and choices make an impact on every person around him. They all want him to succeed and support his goals. It is always up to him to make his goals a reality.

Flash forward to five years from now. Vinnie is passionate about his job that it doesn't feel like a day of his life is work. He has been promoted to chief of police and everyone he works with respects, values, and appreciates him. He has won numerous honorable awards and will be leaving a great legacy. He makes more money than he ever dreamed, and his daughter's relationship with him is more grounded, deeper, and fulfilling.

When we make excuses that are candy coated with the title of "responsibility," we sell ourselves short. Life is way too short to cut corners and play it safe. When we follow our heart and say yes to life, we will be more abundant, successful, and free than we ever dreamed possible. Life gets better when we push through our comfort zones. The famous greats in history never realized their achievements by playing it safe. All of them had to scoot a little outside of their comfort zone and resist society to push to greatness. You have a choice. You can be mediocre, safe, and comfortable, or you can be fulfilled, exuberant, and extraordinary.

Try it out:

1. What is your biggest dream right now? Would you be fulfilled if you achieve it today?
2. What reasons and excuses have you been telling yourself that have prevented you from making this dream a reality?
3. What would it take to make this a reality? How much time? Money? Energy?
4. Create a timeline, using the above factors. Act as if you have all the time, money and energy in the world to make this happen. Stretch it out on paper step by step.
5. Which step can you take right now to work towards this goal?

Embrace Every Opportunity That Comes Your Way

By becoming the yes-master, life will start to open up more opportunities for you. When we say yes to life, life says yes to us. Rather than playing it safe and staying in a comfort zone, I promised myself that for two weeks I would say yes to everything, within reason, of course. I challenge you to do the same thing. Obviously there is no need to break the law or put your life in danger, but say yes to more opportunity at work, say yes to house sitting a friend's vacation home, say yes to signing a contract for something that is important to you, say yes to trying the new spin class. Say, "YES!" Saying yes to things you would normally say no to will open up your world to new possibilities. You will see your world become more flavorful. If you have never eaten sushi because of your fear of raw fish, take yourself on a raw date. Go to a nude beach. Dust off your passport and go on a spontaneous international trip. Round trip tickets to Europe can be less than flying across the United States. Life is short and we must live it fully. By declaring you are a "Yes!" person, things will unfold in front of you. It will be like a magic carpet opening at your feet. As it unfolds, you become the super star. Your life is magnetic, magnificent and full of pizzazz. Like the super stars we see on the red carpet, you will be the person who lights up the room. You will be the center of attention because by experiencing new things you become centered in self. Life rewards us when we play with it. When we choose to try new things, we grow and growing is part of life. The more we grow the more we learn, and the more we learn the wiser we become. Life is enriching and enchanting when we do things we wouldn't normally do.

Awesome Opportunity:

1. For the next 14 days, say, "Yes!" to every invitation and opportunity that comes your way. Watch how your world will change.
2. Write down specific feelings and opportunities that come your way. Document the changes.
3. After the two weeks, look back over your list and decide if living a life in the "Yes!" zone is for you. Try the two-week trial risk free. You have nothing to lose.

Choose Love Over Fear

Excuses are really just cleverly disguised fear-based thoughts. When we tell ourselves, "Oh, I don't have enough money for that goal," what we are really saying is "I fear that I won't have enough to pay my bills if I spend my money on that other thing." We've talked a good deal about fear and how it creeps into our minds to try to rule our lives. Many times we do not even realize our decisions are based on fear.

Think about a situation in your life when you wanted to do something, but you didn't. For me, this has happened a lot. For example, when I was working in the advertising agencies, I was so miserable, the thought of sitting in front of a computer all day chipped away at me like having Jenga blocks being removed from the tower. The longer I stayed in that environment, the more unpredictable and shaky I became. I desperately wanted to leave the corporate world, but I kept telling myself I didn't know what I would do for work if I left advertising. The fear of not knowing where my next paycheck was going to come from stepped in and prevented me from following my heart. I believed that I had to work to make a living so I could pay my bills. I stayed uncomfortably rooted in this vicious cycle. I would look through the window at work and wish I were playing outside. My mind would wander to far-off exotic lands and loving thoughts of all of my deepest desires until I snapped back into reality, I would realize I felt trapped in my current environment, but there was nothing I could do; at least that is how it felt. The thought pattern that kept repeating in my mind was that I didn't have enough money to support myself on another type of salary.

What I didn't realize was, that what was circulating around in my head were really just fear-based thoughts repeating themselves. My biggest fear was not having enough, and it manifested into many different aspects of my life. For example, I often found myself overeating well past the time I was full because subconsciously I feared there was not enough to go around. It was difficult to share with boyfriends, because I feared there wouldn't be enough for me. There was never enough money, enough time, or enough energy. What I really feared was the need to be recognized because I secretly feared that I was not enough.

It is a journey to the heart to discover that you are the source of your own happiness and sadness. Everything in your life is there to help you learn, but, more importantly, everything in you life is there because you put it there. This may be a hard concept to grasp at first, but hang in there for a moment and stay with me. Entertain the idea that life is exactly what we make of it, and every single thing in our existence is there because our higher self or greater good wants us to grow, learn, and appreciate it. When we grow we expand, and when we expand we connect closer to our true self, so naturally when we take on new challenges, or take steps to activating our goals, the little voice in our heads, the fear, gets insanely louder. It screams at us, "Whoa! Warning! Warning! This is uncharted territory!" When we listen to that voice, it keeps us playing small. It keeps us from doing what we were made to do. We all have a right to stand up for ourselves and be, what we are supposed to be but when we listen to the negative voices in our heads we sell ourselves short and stay in a mediocre, static state. You have the choice to listen to the loving, kind voice in your head, or repeat the same negative thought patterns. The human brain can hold one conscious thought at a time, so let's choose a positive thought.

It is our duty to push through the fear and get to the other side. The funny thing about fear is, when we actually look at it dead in the eyes, and say, "Fear, I see you and I am pushing through," it isn't as scary as it looked before we addressed it. When we push through it, it is always more manageable than we made it up to be in our heads. Fear of the unknown is what kept me playing small. I was afraid of not knowing where my next paycheck would come from, for example, but once I learned to recognize that all money is energy as we talked about in Chapter 6, I began to loosen my grip on the future. I slowly recognized that life is truly a journey, not a destination. I looked at my life, at the way things were unfolding, and I recognized my life didn't look like anything I had planned for myself, but it was ten times better. The universe stepped in and helped me create an outstanding life.

I thought I would be the head of the creative department in an advertising agency by age 30, making over $150,000 a year. I was on that track for ten years, pushing uphill. Every day of my life felt like a struggle. I was living in fear. I would have become a creative director if I pushed hard enough, but it was hard work. It was exhausting trying to be someone I wasn't. I was always trying to prove something to others and myself and it got old very fast. I couldn't keep up the charade, so I turned in my big glossy 22" computer and corner office for a quiet spot in the park. Life had better plans for me, and it wasn't until I surrendered to them that I was able to stop pushing.

I stopped trying to be someone I wasn't and now life flows. **Life is supposed to be exciting, fun, and fulfilling.** That is what *Find Your Happy* is all about: declaring you are worth it, and that your dreams do matter. Life is too short to live in fear and choose anything less than outstanding for yourself. If you have a dream, act it out by focusing on loving thoughts and clear intentions. When we get stuck in fear, it paralyzes us and prevents us from moving forward. The first step to busting through fear is to recognize that you have fear. Here are some common fears that keep us from getting what we really want in life. See if any of these ring true for you.

1. Fear of abandonment/ being alone.
2. Fear of failure.
3. Fear of not having, being, or doing enough.

Do you relate to any of these fears? The next step is to ask yourself how these fears keep you from getting what you want. For example, I used to tell myself that I didn't have enough money to quit my job. The fear of not having enough kept me from being in a career that was fulfilling and rewarding.

Now, ask yourself how you benefit from believing in that fear. When we buy into fears, there is always a benefit for us, otherwise we wouldn't listen to the silly voice. Most of the time you end up being right or you feel justified. By believing my fear that there was not enough money, I stayed miserable, but the benefit was I had security. I thought it was security anyway, with the paycheck rolling in every two weeks. It wasn't until I looked at that fear, belief, and benefit that I was able to see the real reason I was buying into it. **If we believe our fears we cannot grow and bust through them.**

The next step is to ask yourself what believing that fear costs. Usually the cost outweighs the benefit but we never give ourselves enough attention to get to the meat of our issues. The cost for me was ultimate self-expression and happiness. In believing my fear, I was depressed, unhappy, overweight and lonely. Most of the time believing our fear keeps us from love, self-love, loving other people, and most importantly, it prevents us from accepting love. Fear is the opposite of love, and we have a choice at every moment in our lives to choose love or fear. Love is kind, loyal, freeing, and bountiful. Fear is everything love is not. When you find yourself in a sticky situation with a significant other or in a situation at work, ask yourself what a loving thing you could do. I started to do this in my relationships and they are deeper, more fulfilling and joyous than I could have ever imagined.

We have two sides to us. There are the dark, devious thoughts that are based on fear and the other side, the expressive, kind, and generous thoughts that come from love. We can choose our thoughts and we can choose love. By choosing love we will expand our horizons and let life flood in. Opportunities will be plentiful.

In a Nutshell:

1. When you say Yes to life situations, more opportunities will come your way.
2. Dreams are patient, but yearn to be realized. You must never give up on them.
3. Following your heart is the most responsible thing you can do.
4. Our job in life is to be happy and being happy means taking risks.
5. Choose love over fear and create miracles in your life.

Additional Resources:

Audio Meditation: *Find Your Happy: Motivational Mantras*, Track 6, "Choose Love over Fear" (available on iTunes, amazon.com, and playwiththeworld.com shop).

Part Two: Take Off

Fearlessly Flaunt the Flawless You

CHAPTER NINE

SPREAD YOUR WINGS

"If you let go a little, you will have a little happiness.
If you let go a lot, you will have a lot of happiness.
And if you let go completely, you will be completely happy." — Ajahn Chah

Take a moment and give yourself a giant bear hug. Wrap your arms around yourself and squeeze tightly because you have made it through Part One and are now ready to literally take off. All of the steps laid out in the first half of the book have led you to this point where you are standing on the ledge and looking out into the vast openness in front of you. Are you ready to fly? You are like a caterpillar turned into a butterfly, and you are poised to fly away from the cocoon and spread your beautiful, colorful wings. This section is all about you, and making your dreams, plans, hopes, and life goals a reality. You can live every moment in a pure state of bliss. You can feel free in every instance in your life even when things are not going as planned. Living a life of fulfillment, freedom, and abundant play is available to you now more than ever before. Unlike other books, processes, or workshops you have taken before, this book has spent a significant amount of time focused on removing the clutter that blocks you from feeling love for life to its fullest. There are barriers that pop up in our minds to keep us from playing the game of life and we have removed those blocks, so salute yourself, hug yourself, and take yourself out, because you did what most people refuse to do in life. You put yourself first and said, "I am worth it; I do want more out of life, and I do have a lot to give." Congratulations! Now the super fun part begins, we get to fly. Now you can literally soar and experience life on unprecedented levels.

Imagine yourself as everything you ever wanted to be. Walk around with your head held high and feel the presence of love flooding through you. You are beautiful and perfect just the way you are. The final step to doing the work, and the first step to flying is to know that you are perfect the way you are and you are enough. By now you may realize that everything you have ever wanted is within you. The power to change your relationships, your job and your outlook on life all begins with you. Being accountable and not accusing or blaming others for your problems can be the single best step to set you free. So let's begin. Are you ready to not just reach new heights, but soar above the world and reach your highest potential? It all starts with a dream.

Dream Big and Follow Through

Having dreams and goals is important to the success of you. When you are working towards something, you feel more useful and fulfilled. When our dreams are realized, we feel a rush of euphoric emotions that is unparalleled by anything else on earth. Think of a dream that has come true for you, whether it was wanting a puppy or getting a good grade on a test, or maybe paying off your car loan. Whatever the dream, big or small, when it is realized you feel more powerful, complete and fulfilled. Loving an enriched life starts with the thought of possibilities, hopes, desires, and wonders in your mind. In order to fly, we need a destination. You can get off the ground and soar, but if you have no clear direction or dream, then you will become tired and bored, and eventually the enthusiasm will burn off. Focusing your flight on a goal will allow you to stay in the air longer. Obviously I am speaking with a metaphor here, but when you fly towards a goal, you will have a purpose.

Awesome Opportunity:

1. Pick one goal that you want to focus on for this month. Write down the goal: *Ex.: Lose ten pounds.*
2. What is one thing you can do today to work towards that goal? *Create a food journal and track all of my calories.*

3. Do this same action for 40 days. (It takes 40 days to truly change your patterns, so commit, focus and watch your life transform.)

Do One Thing Every Day Your Future Self Will Thank You For

Hold yourself accountable. Each day, work towards the big goal by breaking it down into mini day goals. For example, say one of your goals is to lose 10% of your body fat or weigh X amount. This is your big goal. In order to achieve big goals, we must break them down into smaller, more attainable goals. Rather than saying, "I want to lose 20 lbs.," tell yourself, "I will keep a food diary every day this month, I will only eat healthy, fresh foods and I will work out 40 minutes, five days this week." Do this each week, making mini attainable goals, and before you know it your big goal will be a reality.

As I mentioned, in my workshops, I like to recommend that you do one thing every day that your future self will thank you for. Your future self is your best guide and is cheering for you to reach ultimate happiness. When you focus on one thing every day you will be able to reach your goals faster. Rather than stressing about what you did not do, maintain a consistent balance of moving towards your goal with purpose, clarity, and action.

Challenge yourself. Ask yourself what you really want. I always check in with myself and get real honest. I ask, "What one thing do I want right now that I do not have?" Most of the time it is not a material item like a car or new outfit, but a more emotional experience. I want to feel free, or be financially free, or I want to express love in all aspects of my life including the way I talk to myself, because what we do to ourselves we do unto others. If you are constantly telling yourself you can't do it, you're not rich enough, smart enough, attractive enough, etc., you will not be able to attract or get closer to reaching any goal.

We spent a lot of time on negative Nelly talk and it doesn't belong in your life anymore. Starting right now, choose to see the good in every situation, including your dreams. Focus on what you want and the feeling of your dream being a reality. When your brain strays, gently guide it back to kindness and love. Alicia Silverstone, author of *The Kind Diet*, and Kris Carr author of *Crazy Sexy Diet*, have similar philosophies about life.

Both are famous Wellness Warriors and *New York Times* best-selling authors, and they describe this method as the kind diet. They teach the power of kindness as a way of life, providing the power to transform your world by just practicing kindness. What does this mean? Simply treat yourself with only kind, loving and gentle thoughts, words and actions. Do not beat yourself up mentally for anything. Do not talk down to yourself, only practice love and respect for yourself, from the food you eat to the other things you take in. This includes eating food that is fresh, organic and harm free and tuning out negative garbage, media, and negative people who hook into drama and feed off of its negative potions. Remove all news.

Tim Ferris, author of *New York Times* best-seller, *The Four Hour Workweek,* talks about removing all distractions that keep you from living a life in pursuit of your dreams. This means no news, no voicemail and no email. Turn it all off for certain hours of the day. You will see an instant rise in your productivity and you will feel more accomplished every day.

Avoid Dead End Conversations

I do not watch the news and I do not pay attention to headlines or water cooler chat, because it is all distracting and keeps me from reaching my full potential. People tend to group together and fester off of negative energy. Most of the news is negative and most of the population stops 5% before they reach their goals. Coincidence? No such thing. The relationship between reaching your dreams and the amount of distractions you invite into your life is directly proportional. As Tim Ferris says, if news is important enough, you will hear about it.

I also make it a personal choice to avoid the topics of religion and politics. I find that people are very passionate about proving that they are right and the other person is wrong, when in reality, there is no right and wrong. Your duty is to focus on yourself and your goals and live a fearless vibrant life. By avoiding conversations with such heated debate, you can free yourself from wasted time. A dead end conversation is a type of conversation where one or both parties stop listening to the other person, and focus on proving the other wrong. When politics or religion come up, in my experience, it is inevitable that people go gung ho and turn off their ears to open their mouth. Anytime people stop listening, the situation goes into reverse. Whether you are arguing with a significant other, trying to prove a point, or ignoring your inner voice, failing to listening is detrimental to your growth, so rather than spending your precious time on talking and filling each moment up with repetitive arguments and negative thought patterns, try listening.

Be calm and seek your inner voice. It is talking to you all of the time, although people tend to do things to reduce their inner voice. We eat junk food over it (not kind), we get into abusive relationships over it (not kind), we work out over it, we yell over it, spend money over it, watch negative TV over it, get into heated debates over it, when all we really need to do is to quiet ourselves and listen to this gentle, kind voice. It will guide us to where and when we need to be. It is our best friend, helping us make choices to bring us closer to our dreams. When you have a dream, you do not have to worry about how or when it will manifest.

Your job is to be clear about what to dream, and start to work towards it. It does not matter if you do not have enough money to make the dream come true. It does not matter if you do not know where and how you can possibly meet your soul mate when you work and come straight home. The universe and that little voice that we push away is there to guide us, to help us on the right path. A little bit of trust will get us closer to our goals. This is why most people stop before they reach their goal. It becomes too hard, or they can't physically see it manifesting into their reality, so they throw up their hands and say, "I give up!" The other 5% of the population, the ones that wrote that national best-seller, or founded Microsoft, or created Facebook made their dreams a reality by not giving up. In order to fly and soar in your own life, you must choose the path of least resistance and focus on what you want. It may get hard and it will seem tough, but when you give up, you have not tried. You have not reached your full potential, so when you pursue a dream give it everything you have. Only then can you truly see what you are really capable of. Spending your valuable time watching negative garbage will only move you further from your goals.

Awesome Opportunity:

1. Challenge: Do not watch television for an entire week. Extra bonus: for an entire month.
2. Do not engage in political or religious debate or dead end conversations.
3. Rather than watching television, work on your dream list. Plan how much you will need to make your dreams come true. Create an action plan to move towards your desires.

All of the preparation you did in Part One has cleared out space, removed clutter, and eliminated the things that no longer serve you. We did this so you can have a balanced platform to jump-start your future. Spreading your wings is more than just a metaphor. You are really ready to take off, and enjoy life on new levels. Opportunities can now flood to you, and you will see miracles happen every day. You can now enjoy new experiences outside of your comfort zone, in essence, because your comfort zone has grown. When we have a larger area of comfort, our world is more exciting. Things flow more easily, and we often have more opportunities come to us when we are open to receiving them. Because you emptied your cup, there is now room to put what you want into it. Fill it with greatness, playtime, and love. Play with the world every second of the day by honoring yourself and your surroundings.

It all starts with you seeing things in a beautiful light. When we look at the world as a good, happy, and kind place, more good, happy, and kind things can happen and come to us, so open up your arms, stretch high into the sky, and launch yourself into your future. Falling in love with your future never felt easier. Every moment is exciting because we can embrace life and its adversity. This isn't to say that we did all of the hard work so our lives will be easy going from here on out. It means that life's challenges won't seem so complicated anymore. It means we can relax into the hard times as well as the good times. Life is and will always be a roller coaster but when we accept a *Play with the World* attitude, the roller coaster is always a fun ride.

In a Nutshell:

1. In order to reach your goals you need a clear destination. Focus on doing one thing every day that will help you get there.
2. Choose to see the good in every situation.
3. In order to manifest your goal, get rid of all distractions including toxic people who aren't supporting you.
4. When we look at the world as a good, happy, and a kind place, more good, happy, and kind things can happen and come to us.

Additional Resources:

Audio Meditation: *Find Your Happy: Motivational Mantras,* Track 8, "Spread Your Wings" (available on iTunes, amazon.com, and playwiththeworld.com shop).

CHAPTER TEN

BE A KIND JUNKIE

"My religion is very simple. My religion is kindness." — *Dalai Lama*

A kind life is a way of life and a lifestyle that exudes compassion, forgiveness and love. A kind junkie is someone who practices this daily. A Kind Life, coined by peace activist, vegan and actress, Alicia Silverstone, is a way of life that protects, cares for and loves yourself, the planet, and everything on the planet. What does this really mean? When we analyze the kind lifestyle, it is a miraculous way to approach each day because you will be full of love and care. The kind life is nurturing, loving and safe. It starts with recognizing and appreciating the good in the world.

A Kind Lifestyle

If every thought becomes a reality, then why not choose kind thoughts? This is the basic structure of the kind lifestyle. It starts with you and that little voice inside your head. Choose kind thoughts, rather than sabotaging, attacking yourself and others, and casting out negative perceptions, because all of that mental self abuse will pile up and create thick and heavy walls that make it impossible for love to get in. By starting with mini mantras you can be one step closer to living the kind lifestyle. Start out each day with a five-minute me-time. Some people like to call it meditation, visualization or focused intention, but in the *Play with the World* community we call it me-time because, ultimately, all you are doing is getting closer to your true self. You are stepping closer to more love for you.

Upon waking every morning, before setting your feet on the bedroom floor, lie in bed and hold gratitude for all that is around you. Be thankful for the things you do have and then gently hug yourself. Say kind thoughts to yourself. I wake up in the morning and the first thing I say is, "I love you, Shannon, I am so excited for today." I feel the love flood through me and I thank myself for being healthy and being enthusiastic for the new day. Then I say my intention for the day. I say it out loud so the world and my dog can hear me. As my day unfolds, this intention is in focus. Each day's intention is different. One day it could be that I will hold space for others to be inspired. A different day, my intention may be that my diet will be meat and sugar free. Depending on what your goals are, and what your version of happiness is, make a daily intention upon waking up. After giving yourself a hug, embrace the intention and set out on your way. When the day is over, before you fall asleep repeat this five-minute me-time and recap the day's events. Thank yourself for being present and working with yourself to make your dreams come true. Congratulate yourself for something you did. This is not a time to belittle or degrade yourself, but rather to hold space for you to be happy and feel love. If your goal is to lose weight, but you ate ice cream and pizza today, thank the pizza for tasting so good. If you are going to eat food that is high in calories, be excited that you picked the best possible food. Thank yourself in advance for staying on track the next day, and for trying all of the flavors of life.

We are our own worst critics, so when we stray from the kind lifestyle we become bulldozed by negative thought patterns. It is in this moment that we must return to love. We choose to climb our way back to love's kind words. Remind yourself that you did the best you could. Speak to yourself in the same manner as you would talk to a child or a loved pet. Never make yourself feel bad for doing something wrong. Remember there is no wrong or right. Remember you are perfect as you are, so let love in and choose kindness.

The things you take in are just as important as what you release because what goes in must come out. Ask yourself what you have been ingesting lately. What television shows are you watching? What habits do you have that no longer serve you? Are you biting your nails, overeating, picking fights with loved ones, refusing to eat breakfast, or overworking when your loved ones are near? We all have vices, things we do to avoid letting love in. Whether we are behaving like a workaholic, lovaholic or alcoholic, the things we inhale will become the things we exhale. Would you like to walk around ingesting dirty gossip and negative news, or would you rather breathe in light, love, possibilities, and opportunities? This is the difference between saying yes to life and no to negative people, thoughts and situations. Remove yourself from all negative things that no longer serve you. You have a right to be happy and loving, and the negative energies will gravitate towards you when you feed into them.

I refused to accept that we are in a giant recession. I was able to nail a $70,000 position in a society that said there were no jobs. Do not buy into the mumbo jumbo. If a giant trial is on television, let it be. Don't gather around the water cooler to gossip about someone else's lessons. What other people have going on in their lives is something they need to work through. Joining complete strangers to gossip about them will only slow you down in your progress to become your awesome full self. So let it be and leave the drama at the curb.

By embracing the kind lifestyle, you are saying yes to life. You are embracing possibilities and becoming an active participant in your own life. It starts with kindness, so love yourself. Be kind to yourself and share this kindness with the world. What you allow yourself to take in will translate into what you bring into your life. We spent the first portion of the book clearing out space, so now that all of that clutter is removed you have openness to let love come in. As a kind junkie, you can hug yourself and the world with love, passion, and enthusiasm. Be kind to yourself and your neighbor. When you find yourself in a difficult situation — perhaps a significant other is angry and you are on the verge of, or in, a giant argument — choose love. Pick kindness. Challenge yourself to articulate kind words rather than attack, sabotage, or be fearful. By actively focusing on kindness, we can elevate the world. You can change the world. Be kind to yourself. If everything you say or do will be kind, more loving, thoughtful, and generous people will come into your life. Choose love over fear and the kind life will thank you back.

Turn Your Finger Around

Stop pointing the finger. Yes, I am talking to you right now. Where in your life are you playing victim? Where in your life are you blaming someone else and making him or her the source of your unhappiness? Well stop it, right now. I am your inner voice telling you that no good comes from blaming others. When we judge or accuse others of wrongdoing it makes us feel righteous, but it pulls us further away from love's presence, which is completely opposite of being kind. When you refuse to look at all perspectives of each scenario, you are allowing others to make you feel one way or another but we have learned that only you have the power to feel good or not. Rather than blaming others for your unhappiness, look at yourself and ask what you are doing to make this situation things the way they are.

Awesome Opportunity:

1. Think of a challenging relationship and write that person's name down.
2. Ask yourself what is it that is making this relationship so difficult?
3. Ask yourself what am I doing to contribute to this difficult situation?
4. How can I change my mind, mood or response to the situation to be more accountable?
5. Forgive the other person and forgive yourself.

You See Your Reflection in Others

Mothers have a special way of giving us some of the best advice. Whenever a challenging person came into my life, my mother would always tell me, "What you see in others is what you have in yourself." In other words, if you don't like something in another person, most likely you have the same quality in yourself, other people reflect what we think, feel, and do. It used to bug me when she said this, because on some grand level I knew she was right.

I had a friend in 3rd grade who was really mean and always judging other people. I used to tell her to be nice to them, and she would just turn into an angry monster. I never understood how she could be so cruel. It hurt me to see her bully other kids but then my mom told me that she was just reflecting me. I would argue that I was not mean to people. I was the one who offers free hugs. I didn't get it. At school one of the class clowns walked by and mooed at me while I ate my lunch. I immediately felt like a slob. I looked down at my belly and thought, "You are such a roly poly, no wonder you don't have any friends, you are a chub a lub." The realization that I was just like my so-called friend knocked me over. She may have been lashing out and making fun of other people, but this was my internal dialog every day. I was being unkind to myself. I was yelling, sabotaging, and saying hurtful things to myself. Obviously, I was just like her, only the person I hurt wasn't others, it was myself.

I quickly recognized that what we see in other people is a reflection of ourselves, and, by the same token, what you think becomes your reality. So if we are thinking mean, unkind thoughts, then the world will respond in mean, unkind ways. If I was constantly belittling myself and saying such hateful things, then my body began to respond to those thoughts. I would gain more weight, and children would make more fun of me for being the fat kid. Finding kind words to say to myself in a world of bullies was difficult at age nine, but I tried to cope. Rather than lashing out with more mean words, I would lash out with kindness. When we are kind junkies, sticks and stones will never break our bones, and names do not even hurt us because when you practice being kind, the world is less dramatic, less scary and a less threatening place. I recognize now that when people make fun of others, or say something mean to me, I am the one who has the power to give it meaning.

We have already learned that it is never about us. If someone says something that seems offensive, I pause to recognize how I am feeling and then I repeat the thought and ask, "Why did you say this?" Most of the time, the remark was never meant to hurt me directly, but was related to the speaker's own concerns. It is usually something they were thinking about themselves, but because it was on my mind, too, they said something reflecting my inner thoughts, and gave me yet another opportunity to choose love.

Kill Them with Kindness

The adage, "Kill them with kindness," is no fluff. It is a tangible way of improving life. When you choose kind, loving words and thoughts, your actions become kind. People want more compassion in their lives. Every situation is an opportunity to choose love over fear. Kindness will always win over fear. When you practice kindness, you become the rock and stable guide for all of your friends and family. When you choose kind thoughts, others gravitate to you because you glow. I am not talking about kindness routed in manipulation, but rather genuine love and compassion for others. This kindness is untouchable; this kind way of life is a source of true power.

When others say hurtful, derogatory things towards you or another, do not respond in the same manner; simply smile and speak to the positive of the situation. Smile that you know in your heart you are full of love. Because I am a kind junkie I tend to attract people who are negative and mean. In work situations, especially, I have been the target of others picking on me and trying to bring me down. No matter what job I had, it seemed a group of people at work has formed together and in some way "bullied" me. I continued to smile and not take in their unkind words. I would stay positive and see the glass half full. Sure it sucked that they were mean and really rude to me, but it is not about me. I recognize that these people had situations going on in their own lives that they were not happy about. Because I am a happy person, they lashed out on this. Time and time again it has happened but I continue to be true to myself and smile through the adversity.

People have called me "Rainbow Bright," or "Too damn happy," They often mean these names as a compliment, but when they say it, the words are filled with disdain. As far as I see it, there are far worse things to be called than, "Miss Sunshine." You may experience this when you practice the kind lifestyle. People may start to lash out and reject your happiness. The best thing you can do is to continue to be true to yourself. If people you think are your friends get upset when you become happy, then they probably aren't really your true friends. Furthermore, they most likely weren't going to be in your life much longer, so embrace the kind life and love everyone, and everything to the fullest. This includes being kind in the face of negativity. Be kind with your thoughts. Be kind in your actions and what you put out into the world.

Have you ever noticed how smiles are contagious? When you see someone smile, often you can't help but smile back, and then all of a sudden you are smiling at a complete stranger. Then they smile at someone new. All of a sudden the whole place is smiling. Smiling more is one simple way to live the kind life. Becoming a kind junkie is simple. Just choose love, practice kindness and compassion for yourself and others, including animals and the planet. We can't possibly be kind to people and treat animals and nature in a harmful way. Do no harm is the final aspect of living a kind life. This translates into many forms, but basically you choose to disengage from all harmful activities.

This means no more road rage, no more news and television shows filled with celebrity gossip or negative fighting. No more wars (wars are not kind), no more arguing your point is right and everyone else is wrong, no more attacking, judging, or separating yourself from others. No more eating animals that were harmed to go on your plate. The kind junkie lifestyle is a harm-free zone. Embrace it and love your life to the fullest. The kind life is an ultimate goal; if there are some things that work for you and others that do not, then pick what does work for you. I am not advising everyone go out to become tree hugging, vegan peacemakers. I am simply saying to be aware of your thoughts, actions and life, and choose kindness wherever it fits. Being kind will set you free.

The truth is that being kind and compassionate will help tear down barriers between people. Being kind can end wars and stop starvation. Being a kind junkie can change the world. With any kind act, whether we donate money to a charity, start a fundraiser, smile at a stranger or help a blind person cross the street, the intention of doing something nice for another person helps the world. When you do something that is nice and it impacts your family, friends, your community, the environment or world in a positive way, it makes a real difference. The more you practice doing nice things, the better and easier it becomes. When we practice kindness, we train our brains to learn what to think about when we are being nice. When others do nice things for us or when we do something kind for another person it releases endorphins, the chemicals that give off feelings of high spirits, similar to the runners' high experienced by marathon runners. Doing something nice for someone else gives the brain a boost of serotonin, the chemical that gives us the feeling of satisfaction and well being, so why wouldn't we want to do more kind things?

It may seem hard to become a kind junkie in a world of so much negativity. Gandhi said it best, "Be the change you want to see in the world." By starting with yourself, choosing love over fear, and embracing the kind life, you will be inspiring others to do the same. Becoming a kind junkie is one of the most efficient ways to love your life to the fullest.

In a Nutshell:

1. When you remove yourself from all negative things that no longer serve you, you invite good things in.
2. Make me-time. Do mini mantras in the morning for five minutes and in the evening for five minutes.
3. Setting a daily intention will help you reach your goals.
4. Blaming other people for your problems won't solve yours. Be accountable.
5. Other people are a reflection of you.
6. Choose kindness and have an open mind, because it leads to open doors.

Additional Resources:

Audio Meditation: *Find Your Happy: Motivational Mantras,* Track 10, "Listen to Your Body" (available on iTunes, amazon.com, and playwiththeworld.com shop).

CHAPTER ELEVEN

LIVE THE NO-REGRETS LIFESTYLE

"A man is not old until regrets take the place of his dreams." — Proverb

If It's Good, It's Great. If It's Bad, It's Experience.

Victoria Holt's famously said, "Never regret. If it's good, it's wonderful. If it's bad, it's experience." Many people walk around holding onto feelings of anguish, worry, and doubt. These feelings are byproducts of the ever-charged regret. Regret comes from many sources, whether it is a situation that you wish did not happen or something you wish you would have said or done, or even a relationship that you wish you could wipe out of your mind. Regret is a byproduct of fear and remorse and it doesn't belong in the *Play with the World* lifestyle. When you choose to be present in your life, focusing on the moment and creating your dreams, regret does not exist because regret is really only experience. Not all of life's experiences can be good. When they are good, they are great, and it makes sense to enjoy every moment of the highs, but when things happen that we are not comfortable with or wish would have turned out another way, rather than feeling regret, take the opportunity to learn from them. All experiences are lessons; whether they are good or bad, lessons make us grow and teach us more about the world, others and ourselves. Why would regret have any place in a world of wonder?

Your regrets can fall away by thinking about the situation and digging into the heart of it. Let's try it out.

Awesome Opportunity

1. Write down something that you regret in your life.
2. Why do you regret it?
3. Ask yourself what it is about that experience that made it difficult for you to accept it.
4. If things happened the way you wish they had, then how would your life be different?
5. What lesson is there in considering why it didn't happen the way you hoped? What can you learn from this situation?

The thing about regret is it keeps us in a static state. It's a backward-looking, unpleasant feeling. You blame yourself, and wish you could undo the past. Regrets love to make us feel bad. Think about regret as a big bad monster that is trying to manipulate our lives. It wants us to feel bad for things we can't undo because it keeps us living in the past. To break free from this we just need to recognize that regret = opportunity to learn. Learning is exciting and it helps us grow. So all situations in life turn into lessons. It is up to us to choose whether we perceive a situation with love or fear.

Yes, everything comes back to love and fear. Todd B. Kashdan wrote an article for *Psychology Today* called "The Problem With Happiness," about why people are afraid of having regrets. He talks about the fact that we rarely find regret in young children. A seven-year-old makes a comparison about what happened and what might have been and then they move on. They don't dwell on what could have been until they grow older.

In order to feel regret, we have to recognize the consequences of what we did or didn't do. We look inside ourselves to reflect and discover if our actions were a poor choice, or if our mind is creating a situation that is more painful than reality.

For example, I live my life with no regrets. I choose to perceive every situation with an open mind and heart and if something happens that I wish hadn't, rather than referring to regret I see the lesson in the situation. It wasn't always this way. I used to regret many things.

One of my biggest regrets was when I went on a study abroad program to Europe when I was 19. The study abroad was on a ship, called *Semester at Sea*. When the boat docked in Belgium, the principal of the school program threatened that any student who went to Amsterdam would be drug tested and kicked out of the program. Well, all I heard was "kicked out of program," and that was enough for me to steer clear of exploring another country. All of my friends went and I stayed behind in Belgium by myself. It was fine, but when they got back and shared stories of things they saw, heard, tasted, and experienced, I immediately regretted not going because I felt like I missed out. I learned that I listened to authority out of fear of the possibility of getting kicked out.

As it turned out, none of my friends were drug tested and none of them were kicked out of the program. I played it safe, and regretted not taking a risk. Through this experience I recognized that I often put others first and didn't take chances. I thought if I were the good girl, then I would be rewarded. My friends showed me that by taking chances life becomes more rewarding. Living a life of no regrets means taking chances and learning from them. It means loving the good and the bad of life. All of it is part of life, so embrace it fully. Do not push away the bad times, for there is always a lesson hidden within. It will be revealed to us when we choose to see it.

Regret exists because it is useful. When we feel regret because we feel guilty and embarrassed by what we have done, we are motivated to undo the wrongful things we did and make better, more careful decisions in the future. Regret is unavoidable because there are opportunity costs for every choice made. When you select a path, you immediately forfeit other choices and their benefits. By learning to let go of the lack, we can see that there are no wrong choices. Every choice is part of a bigger plan. If you make one choice and grow to regret it, then there is a lesson for you to discover, but if you choose one path and grow from it, the lesson is learned, and your new future can reveal itself. We cannot move forward as fast when we are not learning the lessons. Life on earth is like being in a big classroom. We have lessons of love or hate, of compassion and kindness. When we stay in regret we choose not to do the homework. We do not have an opportunity to pass the course because we are not doing the work. When we do the work, we grow and learn more. Then we progress to the next course. The next lesson awaits, but we must "get" or complete the first one in order to move on.

Let Go of the Past to Enjoy Right Now

Eckhart Tolle, the author of *The Power of Now*, he teaches the power of being in the present moment and releasing fears from the past. It isn't always easy because it is natural for people to create and maintain problems. They give us a sense of identity. We often hold onto our pain far beyond its ability to serve us.

We replay images of past mistakes over and over again in our heads. We allow feelings of shame and regret to shape our actions in the present. Lori Deschene the founder of *TinyBuddha.com*, an empowering website dedicated to simplifying lives and reducing mental clutter, writes about this topic. When we play out regrets in our minds, we cannot move forward. In Deschene's article, "40 Ways to Let Go and Feel Less Pain," she shares, "We cling to frustration and worry about the future, as if the act of fixation somehow gives us power. We hold stress in our minds and bodies, potentially creating serious health issues, and accept that state of tension as the norm." Here are some examples from *Tinybuddha.com* on how to let go of regrets and feel less pain:

- **Change your perception** — see the root cause as a blessing in disguise.
- **Make a list of your accomplishments — even the small ones — and add to it daily.**
- **Feel it fully.** If you stifle your feelings, they may leak out and affect everyone around you — not just the person who inspired your anger. Before you can let go of any emotion you have to feel it fully.
- **Remind yourself that anger hurts you more than the person who upset you** and visualize it melting away as an act of kindness to yourself.

- **Remind yourself these are your only three options:** remove yourself from the situation, change it, or accept it. These acts create happiness; holding onto bitterness never does.

Learning to let go of the past is a powerful way to relax into your life. By learning to appreciate the moment, we can enjoy more opportunities. Numerous studies have been performed to determine the link between happiness and living in the moment. Psychologists at Harvard University collected information on the daily activities, thoughts and feelings of 2,250 volunteers to find out how often they were focused on what they were doing and what made them most happy.

They found that people were happiest when having sex, exercising, or in conversation and least happy when working, resting, or using a home computer. Although the subjects' minds were wandering nearly half of the time, this consistently made them less happy. The team concluded that reminiscing, thinking ahead, or daydreaming tends to make people more miserable, even when they are thinking about something pleasant. By practicing staying in the moment and letting past fears subside, we can settle into our lives more comfortably.

In a Nutshell:

1. Regrets are opportunities to learn and grow.
2. Holding on to anger and resentment hurts you more than the offenders.
3. To enjoy life fully, appreciate the moment and get out of the past and future, be in the present moment for optimal joy.

Additional Resources:

Audio Meditation: *Find Your Happy: Motivational Mantras,* Track 4, "You Make a Difference" (available on iTunes, amazon.com, and playwiththeworld.com shop).

CHAPTER TWELVE

MAKE EVERY DAY YOUR BIRTHDAY

"At the end of life, our questions are very simple:
Did I live fully? Did I love well?" — *Jack Kornfield*

There is something magnificent about the magic energy that swirls around you on your special day. Any day that includes cake and ice cream as a staple and friends lavishly loving you is worth talking about. Your birthday is one day every year that you can count on extra joy flooding in. Even if you hesitate to bump up in age, there is no denying that on our actual birthday it is nice to feel a little more like royalty. Most of us remember what we did for our birthday ten years ago, but we can't even remember what we did last Friday night. It is no secret that birthday celebrations leave a fantastic feeling flooding through our bones, and for most of us it becomes the most memorable day of each year. The secret sauce in birthdays is pure enchantment because the world toasts to you! Love, respect, and hugs are given freely, and you are the center of all the existential goodness. But what about the rest of the lonely, bored 364 days of the years? Excluding holidays, most other days we go about life just making it through. We fall into comfort zones and ripple into boredom. There is a solution to this pouting problem: Make every day your birthday. Let's take a moment to explain why birthdays rock our worlds.

1. It's a celebration of life.
2. We make wishes and dream big.
3. Anything is possible.
4. We take time to play.

5. Family and friends go out of their way to make us feel loved.
6. Food is consumed guilt free.
7. We are more generous with others and ourselves.
8. We spend quality time with loved ones.
9. We sport perma grins the entire day.
10. We appreciate every moment.

After reading through this list, who wouldn't want every day to be their birthday? Whether it's your own birthday or the birthday of someone you care about, the party doesn't need to stop on the actual day of birth. That is the charm of celebrating our awesome life. We can take the same secret sauce of birthdays and apply it to every day of the year. Imagine if you gave a gift to a best friend for no reason, how would they respond? What if you ate chocolate cake for breakfast and left the guilt behind? It sounds pretty fantastic doesn't it? By applying the ten secret powers of the birthday potion to every day of your life you will see a giant transformation in how you live, love, and play. Don't be surprised if you notice how the rest of the world, including all of the people and opportunities around you, shift as well. By simply making small adjustments in your daily patterns, your relationships will be more fulfilling. You will have more self-love, gratitude, and understanding of all of mankind. Like any change in life, it can't happen overnight without intention and focus. Let's rock out each reason together as we dive into the enchanted world of pure bliss.

Celebrate Life

We come into this world protected, safe and secure inside our cozy, gentle mothers; then without warning we are violently thrust through a dark, wet tunnel and pushed into the wide-open light. On top of this there are strangers staring at us, picking and probing. At this moment we realize that life is unpredictable, scary, and not always a safe place. Being born is a significant representation of the ups and downs that will continue throughout our entire life. One moment we feel comfortable, relaxed and untouchable, and then out of nowhere we are laid off, find out a close family member has cancer, or the spouse we thought was the love of our life wants a divorce. There is no running from the reality that life will always deliver peaks and valleys. Life is not always easy, but that is precisely why it is so precious.

The majority of life's best rewards are possible only because of the hard work, the push and pull of the difficult times. If life were an easy, breezy joy ride, then most of us wouldn't appreciate happiness or understand real fulfillment. There is no better time to honor the trials and tribulations of our own life than on a birthday. On that one day of the year, we forget about all of the drama that lurks in our shadows. All of the stress slithers away and we relax into the peaceful knowing that everything is always going to be okay. On birthdays we lighten up and laugh as we find comfort in the little things. It is a day we recognize that we do live in a beautiful world and life is so precious. By taking a few moments every day to be thankful for the beautiful things in our lives, despite any dramatic events, we can move ourselves closer to a state of constant happiness. When we are happy, we enjoy life more, and let's face it, no one likes being around a cranky pants. It's no coincidence that on our birthday people flock to us and want to party along side the perma-grinned beauty. We are happy and like attracts like. Naturally, people want to be around happy people, so even when times are tough, shine light on the awesomeness that surrounds you.

Whether you spend extra time petting your dog or cat, or you hold the door for a stranger, or let someone else in front of you on the freeway, little gestures will span a long way. The ripple effect is infectious, and pretty soon, one small act of kindness and celebrating life will transform your entire day. But what is a celebration without a party? If you are feeling really gutsy why not throw yourself a "HAPPY DAY" party? Birthday parties aren't the only times we should shake our moneymaker, so why not throw a "Surprise! Our life is rad!" bash in the middle of winter? The point of all of this is to move outside of our heads and appreciate life and all it has to give. Humans tend to get stuck in a negative thought process that derails our hopes and dreams, but on that one special day every year, we remind ourselves to smile. We laugh more and play with loved ones. By actively connecting with the feelings of love, gratitude and joy, we can elevate our life experience and celebrate life every day.

Make Wishes

Every birthday, the candles come out and the wishes want to play. As the dreams pop to the surface, we blow out the flames with the secret ambition to see our deepest desires realized. Why do we dream bigger on our birthdays? There is no reason we can't apply this same optimistic, positive, and powerful potion into our daily routines. I started doing this on my birthday by taking the age I just turned and making that many wishes. So when I turned 28, I made 28 wishes. I wrote them all down and sealed the piece of paper with a kiss. Miraculous things can happen when we state our intentions out loud. The energy that we use when we make a wish on our birthday is the same powerful stuff we can use to create an awesome opportunistic life throughout the year. A year later I pulled out my wish list, and 25 out of the 28 wishes had come true.

Our dreams do want to come to life. They are like plants; we must feed them, tend to them, let them grow. But if we never even plant the seed, how are we supposed to enjoy the garden? Maybe I am being too metaphorical here, but you should be able to get my gist that dreams belong in our lives. When we wish upon a star, we do more than just connect with our childhood imagination.

In fact, when we set goals and then achieve them (even seemingly small ones) we raise the dopamine levels in our brain. High NE levels are associated with feelings of joy, excitement, and even euphoria. By making wishes and setting goals you can experience an outrageously cool aura. I no longer reserve wishes for my birthday. They come out to play every day. Every morning when I wake up, the first thing I do is smile and set an intention for my day. By making a morning wish, I can focus clearly throughout the day and stay in the realm of possibilities.

The article, "Definitions of Goal Setting," on the website *www. livestrong.com*, writer, Edwin Locke, professor emeritus at the University of Maryland School of Business, created a goal-setting system that can be used by both individuals and organizations. According to Locke, the most effective goals are specific and challenging. Vague goals leave you wondering whether or not you have achieved them, while easy goals fail to gratify you with a sense of accomplishment. Write down what you'd like to accomplish. This is a critical step that most people forget to do.

By writing your goals down on paper you send a message into the universe that says, "I desire this." Without sharing your hopes and dreams they cannot move forward. The power of intention is set forth when we share our hopes and dreams. Whether you discuss your goals with your loved ones, or simply write them down on a piece of paper in a personal notebook, the results will astound you.

As I mentioned previously, I make vision boards for my goals. Rather than New Year's resolutions, I make intentions. With each intention, I create a vision board, a collage of images and sayings that inspire me. If you really want to jump-start your wishing wonderland, then host a dream board party. Invite your favorite people over and have a positive-paste party. Everyone brings their favorite magazines, you supply the rocking tuneage and space, and people start to paste away. Within an hour you will see versions of the best you, your best life, and your hopes, along with your best friends' dreams visualized into reality. If the proof is in the positive pudding then why not make a daily intention? Why not set a goal and work towards it? The sky is the limit when it comes to our dreams. One of my favorite quotes is by W. Clement Stone. "Aim for the moon. Even if you miss, you land among the stars."

One common pitfall in setting goals is not paying attention to how they make you feel. When we set goals, we should be getting butterflies in our stomach. If you feel nauseous or frustrated then perhaps it is time to check in and get honest about why you set that goal. Be careful to ensure that you are not setting someone else's goals for yourself. Your goals should reflect what you really want, not what you believe you should want, or what someone else tells you that you want.

This is precisely what happened to me. I thought I wanted to live in the big city, and work at a giant advertising agency. I was relentlessly pushing towards this perception of what I was determined would make me happy. But I never once checked in with myself to ask whose goal it was? I thought I wanted to be in advertising, but I quickly learned that the fancy loft and shiny shoes weren't made for me. After suffering a deep depression I came out of Chicago with clarity about what I really wanted. I made daily goals to push my way out of my own fear. I wrote intentions on my bathroom mirror with red lipstick. Pretty soon, I had lost 15 pounds, completed a triathlon and become a published author.

These goals felt right to me. In fact they made my heart sing. If your goals don't leave you twitterpated then it's time to break up with those goals.

Otherwise, even the most skillfully framed goals will fail to inspire you. After all, there is no point in mustering your internal resources to go to a place you don't want to be. Psychologist Judith Sills, author of *The Comfort Trap,* advises people to create an internal vision that excites them. If the idea of meeting your goals makes your heart beat faster, you're on the right track. Rather than keeping wishes to one day a year, try blowing out a candle every day. Quite possibly you will also blow yourself away with all of the opportunities and dreams realized.

Anything Is Possible

There is no escaping the reality that each day we get one day closer to the next age. As the next decade approaches, childhood fantasies fade away, and we hunker down into the adult realities of life. Responsibilities consume our decisions, and we are often left exhausted and anxious. Whether we celebrate someone else's birthday or our own, we take time out for each other. We celebrate together and help add joy into each other's lives. On birthdays, life seems expansive and exciting. We make plans; we invite our loved ones to parties. The sky is the limit for what we want to do, and anything is possible. For my 30th birthday I asked myself what do I really want to do? If I could do anything in the world, what would I do? I love family and friends, so a giant party was a must. I also love travel, adrenaline-inducing activities, and doing girly stuff like shopping, and spa time. My possibilities were endless. I scheduled a month-long celebration to make the most out of my special day. My plans included a big bash with 30 of my closest friends and family, a makeup makeover, a spa weekend with three hours of perfect pampering, a shopping spree, skydiving, and a trip to Brazil. All of these started as tiny inclinations, small possibilities that only existed inside my head, but I daydreamed and let myself enjoy the process of thinking about the ifs.

One of the biggest dream killers of all is when we won't allow ourselves to want what we really want because we can't see a way for it to happen. Think back on your life. How many times have things happened differently than you originally thought or planned? Most of the time it turned out in an even better way than you ever imagined. You couldn't have orchestrated it better had you planned every second of it with exact precision. Your dreams are in your heart for a reason. Not everybody wants the same things. There are plenty of dreams to go around. The good news is possibilities never end. You are granted the power to make dreams come true when you dare to dream the dream. You just have to find that power, believe in yourself and your dream, and go for it. Often, we do not need to know how it will happen, but thinking about possibilities and enjoying the process gets us into a positive mindset, which in turn allows more good things to come to us. Anything is possible in this life. Using the same energy we put into planning how our birthday will unfold can easily be applied to every day of our lives. Every achievement will build upon the last achievement and soon you will know you are unstoppable, that you have the power to make your every possibility come true.

Take Time to Play

Playtime is synonymous with fun, yet as adults we don't always make time to have fun. Think about when we were children and everything was enchanting. Even sitting in the yard playing with the rocks was more fun than watching TV. For many of us, when we grew up work became a chore, and we were often so burnt out at the end of the day that we zombied out in front of YouTube. But when birthdays came around we found fun things to do. Whether it was trying a new restaurant or going to a concert, or just buying a new outfit, we tend to have more fun and enjoy the process of playing.

Have you ever caught yourself saying, "I don't have time for fun, I have work to do," or, "I have too many other things to worry about, why worry about having fun?" The reasons we need to have more fun in life are obvious. When we play we reduce stress, we worry less and feel more connected with our true self.

If the rewards are so obvious, then why don't more people take time out to play? We become so stuck in the patterns and stresses of life we forget to play. We focus on our problems rather than solutions. By shifting our mind set to include a daily dose of play, we can begin to lighten our load and smile a bit more. When we play, we let go of our problems, even for a short while, and then they become less intense. Playtime (or relaxation) gives us time to adjust, time for contemplation. So many people get their best ideas in the shower because when your brain is not focused on one thing in particular it's free to wander, sometimes bringing new insight and understanding. When we play we live in the moment. We get out of our own head and focus on the fun. Smiles and laughter fill the moment rather than stress, anxiety and worry. When problems seem overwhelming, it's the little things that can help make them seem more approachable.

One way to encourage yourself to play more is to write down things you enjoy. To make it more fun, I like to list a number of activities equal to my age. Treat the list like a free write and you may surprise yourself as I did. I saw that the majority of the things I love to do are related to the outdoors. I love doing fun things like hiking, cycling, running on the beach, camping etc. I wondered when was the last time I had actually gone outside to enjoy nature? It had been over four months, so making this list became my wake up call. It served as a gentle reminder that I need to get out and play for my sanity.

I posted the list where I could see it on the fridge. That way if I was craving something, I would see the list and remind myself that what I was craving might not be in this cold icebox. So what do you have to lose? Make a list of things that sound fun. Have you ever wanted to take a cooking class or learn a new language? The possibilities are endless when you go to your heart and ask it what it wants. This is a simple exercise to help us get back to the things that matter most to us. It shouldn't feel like another chore. Just simply ask, "What do I love to do?" and then go do it.

Many times when we want to do something people and situations come into our lives that help us get what we want. Did you ever notice when you are thinking about getting something new, like a new car or a new pet, you start to see them everywhere? I wanted a new Jeep so bad that it's all I could think about for a few weeks. One day I was sitting at a stoplight and there was a Jeep Wrangler on every side of my car, one in front, one behind me and one on both sides. I laughed out loud thinking it was some cosmic joke, but it was a simple mirror reflecting my inner thoughts. That's the same way the list works. If you make a list of things you love to do, then you will be one stop closer to actually doing them.

Maybe you love to cook, so you put it on your list. The next day you are at the store and you may see a flyer for cooking classes or a great cookbook on sale. Things will work out and align for you when you make it an intention to have fun. By taking the same focus we put into making sure to have fun on our birthdays into our every day life we will see dramatic changes in our lives. Not only will we smile more, have less stress, more energy, and even more friends but we will be happier and more fulfilled.

Think about when we were children and recess was part of the school day. Taking time to play is so important that national school system put it into the curriculum. Recess is a time for reflection, a time of laughter, fun and play. As adults, through no fault of our own, recess has been pushed to the back of our lives. As we have far off daydreams of one day making it to that exotic location, play in that moment seems as unrealistic as Elvis rising from the dead. Recess is fun, but adulthood doesn't have room for fun, so why not take a life recess? An old coworker would stand up from his desk and say, "I need a life recess," and then take a break when he got stressed at work. I found this idea fabulous because a recess is just a moment of play added into each day. Let's all make recess part of every day.

Go Out of Your Way to Make Others Feel Loved

Someone told me once that you know who your real friends are on your birthday and when you move. People who wish you a happy birthday and who make time to spend with you on your special day are people worthy to be in your life (and the same is true of people who help you move). If someone forgets to wish you a happy birthday, or doesn't invite you to their party, then they are more than likely a superficial buddy. Part of this section is all about getting rid of superficial snobs and recognizing the goddess or god that you truly are. Birthdays are the one day every year when it is all about you. Friends and family will help you feel like queen/king for a day, so let them lavish you with lovely love. However, all too often when it is not our birthday, we usually let relationships slide.

When was the last time you spent quality time with your friends? What about your parents? When was the last time you shared a good meal with them? Many of us get a job, sometimes moving away from our family and closest friends, and we get caught up in the routine of work. But on birthdays, they always come back around, take us out to dinner, give us a genuine phone call and leave positive messages on our Facebook wall. All of the love being flung around is one of the best parts of birthdays. Not only do we feel more loved, but we feel special and appreciated. Think about how you treat your friends on their birthdays. We usually buy them presents, flowers, a nice card with a sentimental message, not to mention that we give them extra hugs and attention. I always wonder why we do these awesome things on birthdays, but most other days of the year, we are canceling plans, not sharing how we feel with each other, and buying flowers only when we want to apologize.

The way we show up for others on birthdays is the same way we should show up for our friends and ourselves on every other day of the year, being generous, kind, respectful, and open to possibilities. Life will be more enriched if we take little steps to make each other feel appreciated every time we see each other. Whether it's embracing for a little bit longer or treating a friend to a coffee on your coffee date, it is the little things that make the biggest difference. Perhaps give your mamacita a call and tell her how much she means to you. Invite your pops over for a home-cooked meal. The goal is to reconnect with the relationships that we let fall behind. At the end of our lives we will not remember the places we worked or how much money we made, but we will remember how we made other people feel and how they made us feel. We will recall the imitate connections we made and how deeply we loved. Life is about our relationships and tending to them every day is one of the best ways to live an enriched life.

Eat Food Guilt Free

When we are little, we would eat until we were no longer hungry, even if it was a piece of cake dripping with succulent chocolate sauce. We look at that sweet treat and dive in with joy. Most often we would stop shy of finishing the whole piece in order to quickly get back to playtime. Back then, our stomachs and brains united to signal we were full. For many of us, somewhere along the way, emotion stepped in and hooked up with hurt feelings and eating became not only a social activity to mask feelings, but an intimate act of self-sabotage. Then the media comes in and paints beautiful skinny people all over the magazine covers and TV screen. Women are often confused, scared, and frustrated that we eat more. It doesn't take a doctor or scientist to see that western culture is in an epidemic of grave proportions.

I am not a dietitian or a doctor, but I know from experience that extra weight on people is a direct reflection of a deeper issue that needs a little love and cuddle time. Over the past 15 years my weight has fluctuated up and down as I struggled, tortured, and self-sabotaged myself to gain and lose the same 40 pounds. I have always been an extremely active person, competing in triathlons and endurance sports all around the world, but my love of food has been something that screamed for a little attention. I would tell myself just because I worked out so hard I could eat more. Every time I ate that cookie dough ice cream I felt guilty and dissatisfied that I was "caving" in, but one day of the year, every birthday, I would leave my guilt at the door.

If you are like me, then birthdays are a free pass to enjoy everything and anything, and to live life fully. For me, this usually includes indulging in generous slices of gourmet pizza, followed by creamy sweet ice cream and cake. One thing different about this day is that I don't feel guilt. I embrace the food and welcome it in, and rather than gluttonous, stuffed fortification, it becomes an intimate act of self-love. I thank my food for being part of my birthday; I love it and appreciate its nourishment and, oddly enough, sometimes I find that I don't actually finish the entire piece of cake. More often than not I stop at one piece of pizza. This year it occurred to me how nice it felt to enjoy my food.

I have spent the majority of my life running from food and feeling bad if I eat it because it is obviously going to go to my thighs. After I spent my entire 30th birthday eating whatever I wanted when I wanted, I realized that I didn't actually eat as much. I stopped when I was full. I didn't inhale my crème brulee, but rather embraced its soft, sweet, creamy texture. I had a couple bites then I was done. I enjoyed and welcomed it, and my old pal, guilt, didn't even try to crash the party. He was nowhere to be found because the pity party was nonexistent. I thought I might be on to something here . . . this whole eating guilt free could be a better way to live.

On my deathbed, what do I want to remember? It won't matter what the number on the scale is or the fact that I obsessed for the majority of my life over losing and gaining the same damned ten pounds. I don't want to be the person who wastes my life refusing the beautiful flavors of earth. The rich, bountiful textures are created to be consumed. It was as if something clicked inside of me, and I refused to be that person who felt guilty anymore. Maybe fear of wasting my life, worrying about the things I can't control was really about me denying myself the simple pleasures. I would feel so guilty that I pushed food away, and then when I would give in, I would eat so much, and eat so fast, that my belly would feel like it had to burst.

I went through phases of binge eating, then purging, and then another phase of three-week fasts eating nothing but a couple grapes a day, and maybe a Starbucks. None of my diets worked. None of the books I read helped. I didn't want to be the person who refused a piece of gum because the five-calorie intake would have put me over my daily budget. I was exhausted and at my version of rock bottom. I didn't want to go through life feeling bloated, uncomfortable and ugly, so I changed my mind. I woke up and said, "I accept myself. I love myself and I love this food."

I started to treat my food with respect. I educated myself on the horrific things that go on in the meat industry, and I made the switch to an organic, cage-free and pretty much a vegetarian/vegan lifestyle. I started cooking more and putting love into every slice of the vegetables. I juice in the morning for breakfast and I don't obsess over my workouts. Now, I work out until it is no longer fun. After 45 minutes if I feel complete, I stop running. Nothing is off limits anymore. Every food is fantastic, and guilt is no longer part of my feeling vocabulary. By adopting this lifestyle, the weight that I struggled to lose for half of my life has gradually just fallen away. I accept myself and love myself fully. Food is energy and it is something we all need. I appreciate the food for what it is. Food is just a source of nourishment and life.

I have a new rule that if it isn't good, I don't eat it. After my first bite, I decide if I want to fill my body with something I don't like. If it tastes bad, it doesn't go in my god pod. Our bodies are our temples. By eating whatever we want without guilt, we can love ourselves fully and embrace all that life has to give. What you may discover is that the cravings for the sweet, salty stuff will subside. That is why I can eat a piece of cake and have one bite. It's no longer about trying to fill a void. I am completely confident and comfortable with whom I am. The same way we enjoy food on our birthday is the magic recipe for a happy, fulfilled and comfortable life.

Be More Generous

The majority of the year, I am on a tight budget, refraining from buying extra stuff. I have actually refused dinner invitations from friends because of my desperate attempt to save money, but every year around my birthday I lighten up a little and let money flow more effortlessly. When I see a cute shirt, I usually buy it, telling myself it's my birthday present to myself. Sometimes I treat myself to my favorite ice cream, guilt free. For the past few years, I have taken myself on vacations. When birthdays occur, generosity usually comes out to play. Every time a friend has a birthday, I give without hesitation because it is fun to see their face light up. I bring the same joy to myself when I buy myself goodies, but I usually don't treat myself with the same respect the other 364 days of the year. Generosity is a pathway to self-fulfillment. When we give, we feel good. Being generous means treating each person as though they have already achieved their potential for greatness. It is a token of appreciation that often reflects a sincere desire to make others' lives easier or more pleasant.

There are simple ways to apply a giving attitude to every day of your life.

1. Notice little things you can do to help make the lives of the people you interact with easier and more enjoyable. I used to bring my boss coffee every Friday. I sometimes leave love notes in obscure places for my significant other. Little things that make a world of difference in another's eyes can help.
2. Extend this thoughtfulness to strangers. Smiling at a stranger holding a door open for the person behind you, or letting another car in front of you when driving are all small acts that can make a big difference.
3. Generosity is not always monetary. It could be cooking a nice dinner for your friends, or forgiving a person who made a mistake. All you have to do is tap into the sweet feeling that generosity brings and feed the love because what goes around comes around. Being friendly to yourself and others makes you feel good, but more importantly it comes from a place of love, and love is the fruit of life.

Spend Quality Time with Loved Ones

Every birthday is filled with compassionate hugs and generous words. People often come out of the woodwork to make you feel special. Why wouldn't they? You are the superstar and deserve every bit of love lavished. Why do we reserve one day of love when we care about these people all year around? Sure, we meet up with friends, visit our parents, and spend time with our siblings on occasion, but more often than not, the workload creeps in and our own mini dramas stop us from spending quality time with loved ones. By making time to see friends and family, we not only feel better about ourselves, but we relax and feel better about our day. When we have a day that is well spent, we sleep better and have lower levels of stress. The reality is that life takes over and we get swamped with responsibilities. Many households need two incomes just to make ends meet, and parents, friends, and family feel out of balance at the end of the day. Making time for loved ones is one of the best ways to wean off stress. When we actively make time for one another, our connections grow stronger. We feel more connected and closer to each other. We sport perma grins the entire day.

One of my favorite songs is the 1988 Bobby McFerrin hit, "Don't Worry, Be Happy," The lyrics say:

> *In every life we have some trouble*
> *When you worry you make it double*
> *Don't worry, be happy*
> *Cause when you worry*
> *Your face will frown*
> *And that will bring everybody down*
> *So don't worry, be happy (now) . . .*

I love this song because of the simple message. Don't worry, just be happy. It is hard to not feel good on your birthday. Even if you are a person who dreads the next year, the actual birthday is almost always a blast. We smile all day and love every second of it. The little worries that bothered us yesterday seem so far away on our birthday. We smile and laugh, and genuinely have a good time. By adopting the perma grin every day we will feel more connected to ourselves. Bobby McFerrin says when we worry we make it double, so just don't worry. Life is as complicated as we make it. No need to stress more. Smile and watch your entire world feel lighter.

I started doing this when I felt really angry and stressed out. I simply forced myself to smile. It felt uncomfortable at first but the experience forced me to take a step back and see my anger for what it was, a fleeting emotion that will always come and go. When I smiled, I had to laugh out loud at how silly and awkward it felt. The saying, "Fake it until you make it," made sense for me. I was faking happy until it felt comfortable, and this process really helped open up my emotions. I simply pushed my way through anger with a gentle smile and within time the smile warmed the entire day. My smile has saved me on many occasions. It really just reminds me to be happy and that everything is always okay. Smile more to feel happy and free.

Appreciate Every Moment

Blowing out the candles on a birthday cake is the sweet spot to every birthday. It makes the day more memorable as we dream of our wishes and put them into a magical blow. With one release, we hope they come true. The magic of blowing out the candles is more than just the wish, it is because we are in the moment. When we live in the moment, we are mindful and present in the fullness of life. Most of the time we fall into the habit of simulating a robot, automatically living out habitual patterns of self-pity, anger, lack of fulfillment, fear, etc. These habitual tendencies take over and run our lives for us, often without us being able to stand back and decide whether this is what we actually want to be doing. It can be a real shock when we start to realize just how habitual and automatic our lives are. When we realize how much runaway thinking leads to states of suffering. When we're in this robotic state, we're not mindfully aware of what's going on.

Being in the moment is just another way of saying that we are aware of what is going on in our experience, that we are not just being angry (or whatever) but are aware that we are angry, and are aware that we can choose to be otherwise. With everything in life we have a choice, and we can choose to be happy if we want. By living in the moment, life becomes more fulfilling, rich and rewarding.

In a Nutshell:

1. Being more generous will help you feel more abundant.
2. Spending quality time with loved ones will help you feel more happiness in the moment.
3. Appreciate the moment to feel more peace.
4. Add more "birthday" into your daily routine.

Additional Resources:

Audio Meditation: *Find Your Happy: Motivational Mantras,* Track 9, "Appreciate the Moment" (available on iTunes, amazon.com, and playwiththeworld.com shop).

CHAPTER THIRTEEN

THINK BIG, ACT SMALL

*"Happiness comes when your work and words are of benefit to yourself and others." — **Buddha***

Altruism and Happiness

Altruism is the belief in, or practice of, disinterested and selfless concern for the well being of others. It means being kind to others without expecting anything in return. We spent some time understanding the benefits of being kind. Giving without expecting anything in return is a huge part of being a kind junkie.

PBS.org, dedicates a section of their website called "The Emotional Life" to topics such as "Altruism & happiness." Altruistic acts — including kindness, generosity, and compassion — are keys to the social connections that are so important to our happiness. Research finds that acts of kindness, especially spontaneous and out-of-the ordinary acts, can boost happiness in the person doing the good deed. Being generous leads to many good things. Being helpful to others can help us feel happier.

Giving does not always involve spending money. People can also give their time, energy, or simply even for listening. When we spend time helping others our mood can improve. Think about someone you know who is very kind and generous with his or her time. Their generosity often leads to more generosity.

When we see images of people helping less fortunate people who are affected by natural disasters or poverty, disease, etc., we want to reach out to help. Seeing others helping tends to make us want to give more as well. By giving you can create a ripple effect of more good deeds. It is like a smile from the heart, passed along to help create a better world. Being kind can start a chain reaction of positivism; being kind to others may lead them to be grateful and generous to others, who in turn are grateful and kind to others.

There is a difference between someone who gives without expecting anything in return, those who give expecting something back, as well as those who give because they think it will make them a "good" person. When we give there is an energy that is exchanged, and the giver is always the one who receives greater benefits. Volunteers often see greater benefits than those they are serving, but when someone is wrapped up in wondering what is in it for them, the energy is shifted. The receiver has a difficult time receiving the full capacity from help. Understanding that when we give, we get so much more will often trigger us to want to give more.

Recently I had the opportunity to go to Jamaica to cover the Caribbean Yoga Conference. During the conference, a group of us visited the SOS Children's Orphanage to volunteer our time and teach the children yoga. I was ecstatic to go! I remember thinking on my way there how much of a difference we would be making for these children. We would be teaching them yoga, and the power of breath and movement, but in my experience I got so much more in return. It wasn't about me helping them at all. They helped me. The children taught me how to be present, how to appreciate the moment, and how to laugh at the silly things in life. It was one of the most profound moments of my life, and I feel honored to be one of the only journalists to cover the event.

There Is Always Something You Can Do

On March 11, 2011, I woke up excited because it was my birthday. I welcomed in the beautiful, fresh, new day. The TV was on, and as I walked downstairs I saw that a giant tsunami had hit the coast of

Japan and wiped out cities and towns, leaving thousands missing. My birthday happiness changed from a euphoric rush to devastation in an instant. All I could think was how could I help? I listened to the strained screams of victims; I saw dogs drowning and homes turned upside down. Suddenly my having a day all about me because it was my birthday became unimportant.

Many people experienced the same horror in watching the events unfold on television and also felt helpless. The situation seemed so far removed from us in our cozy homes in America that many felt numb to the tragedy. I spoke to many people who said, "I feel helpless; there is nothing I can do." Trust that there is always something we can do. I recognized that I could make a difference, so I started a fundraising campaign to help raise money to help the victims. I went to Mercy Corps and created my own fundraising page. I asked people to donate to my campaign rather than buying me birthday presents. I took action and did something. Even though my efforts were small, I could make a difference and I did. After raising $100 for the Japan Relief Efforts, the head of Mercy Corps sent me a personal thank you and a certificate of appreciation. When I opened up the certificate it was a gentle reminder that my friends and I had made a difference. Together we raised more than $100 dollars. That is better than zero dollars, and it went to help people less fortunate than us. There is always something you can do and it starts with asking yourself, "How can I help?"

Being of service to others is one of the highest forms of enlightenment. When we serve others we recognize that we are part of a greater plan. We see that everyone is connected and that is why the *Play with the World* mentality exists. It is not just about adventure, play, and fun. Sure, that is a big part of it, but underneath it is about recognizing that our own lives matter and seeing that we are connected to a greater plan. Every single thing you do affects another person. We are all one. Sometimes it takes world tragedies to bring us together.

To see another person connected to you is an easy way to offer help. No one is any different. When we remove all of the different hair colors, skin colors, weight, clothes, and personalities, we are all the same. We all want love; we all want to make a difference and feel connected to life. We need each other to get to where we want to go. So when you think about your goals and your personal dreams, recognize that they are not just for yourself, but also for the world. Every single thing you say and do has an impact and is part of the plan. By giving more we receive more.

Little Things Make the Big Difference

Sometimes the little things are all that matter. The little things we do for another person are often bigger and better than the things we do on a grand scale. Opening a door for a stranger, buying your friend lunch unexpectedly, taking out the garbage when your significant other is tired from the day, picking flowers to put in a vase to liven up your room, buying ointment for that rash that has been irritating you — all of these may seem small, but the effects are plentiful. Taking care of yourself and doing small things for yourself is just as important as helping others and the bigger things we do. Troubling or annoying situations slow us down. Buying cream for a rash you keep ignoring, or replacing a desk chair that has been causing a chronic backache will remove these deterrents. It is in the details that life can flow. By focusing on the details and the little things, we can open up space and remove negative influences. By starting with you, the ripple effect can move outwards.

For example, I had been having horrible stomachaches and groggy, fuzzy headaches that felt like migraines for a few weeks. I woke up feeling hung over. I realized I was not drinking enough water, and had been consuming massive amounts of sugar. I had been celebrating birthdays, weddings, anniversaries, and family reunions. It seemed every day was another reason to go crazy and love the sugar. When I woke up, I realized that the actions I took the previous day were affecting my current day, so I worked on being present and taking care of myself in the moment, especially the little things, like making sure I drank more water. I started a detox program and became more conscious of what I put in my mouth once again.

Our bodies are able to tell us what is going on. The way our body feels is the best indicator of how we are treating ourselves. How we treat ourselves is how we treat others and the world. If you are constantly feeling sick, tired, or depressed there is a reason. Our bodies reflect and show what is really going on behind the scenes. What we do to our bodies is what we do to the world. Furthermore our bodies are the best show and tell for how we are relating to the world.

Awesome Opportunity:

1. Check in with your body, how do you feel right now?
2. What actions did you take today to create this current mood?
3. If you don't like the way you are feeling, ask yourself why your body is reacting this way. What is it trying to show you?

For example, maybe you get headaches often and you also drink mounds of caffeine. If you go a day without drinking your coffee, you may experience a "caffeine headache." Our natural reaction is to go get caffeine to improve the way we're feeling, but it is most often our body's way of saying, "Please stop drinking so much caffeine." We mask our feelings and emotions with things, and the majority of the time our bodies become the real victim.

Self-help authors and my dear friends, Christine Arylo and Gabrielle Bernstein, lead a seminar series called the "Fear Cleanse." In the course, students learn about the body and its intention in the world. Most people abuse their bodies. Getting honest about how we use our own bodies is an essential step in seeing how we are connected to the greater good.

Some common ways we abuse our body are using it as a punching bag when we beat it up mentally, making it our slave, exhausting, and overworking it. We neglect it, forget about it, and don't take care of its basic needs. We treat it like a garbage can by dumping garbage in it and making poor food choices. Sometimes we whip it into shape, by working out extra long or going commando on ourselves. All of these examples are shared in the "Fear Cleanse" workshop. I share them with you here because what we do to ourselves, we do unto others. If we are not taking care of ourselves, then giving to others and the world will be a wasted effort. We must first take care of ourselves and treat ourselves with respect and admiration, or no amount of giving in the world can fill up the void.

Awesome Opportunity:

1. Ask how you are currently mistreating your body.
2. Write down the answer.
3. What is this trying to teach you?

A good exercise is to recognize that everything our bodies do is a reflection of what we are currently thinking and doing. Our human bodies are the fastest indicator that something is wrong. By learning to recognize our bodies as a tool for guidance we can open up the possibilities to enjoy life more. When our body needs to rest, we can give it rest. When our body is in pain, ask, "Why is this part of my body aching?" Louise Hay, author of best-selling, self-help, spiritual book, *You Can Heal Your Life,* makes a direct comparison between bodily illnesses and the thought patterns that created them. Every disease is really "dis-ease" and we have the power to reverse it with our actions and energy. By focusing on being intentional and deliberate, we can start the ripple effect in quick order. When we try to be there for other people but we are neglecting ourselves, and the energy exchanged is weakened. Therefore, before we give we must always make sure we are taking care of ourselves first. When you put yourself first, the rest of the world can find balance within your balance. To find balance you must give and get, starting with treating yourself kindly and listening to your body.

In a Nutshell:

1. Giving does not always involve spending money. Be creative with how you give.
2. There is always something you can do. It starts with asking yourself how you can help.
3. Listen to your body. It will tell you everything you need to know.
4. All disease and discomfort is a manifestation of a thought pattern in your mind. Choose positive thoughts.

CHAPTER FOURTEEN

MAKE MOTHER NATURE YOUR BFF

"Knowing trees, I understand the meaning of patience.
Knowing grass, I can appreciate persistence." — *Hal Borland*

Nature Is a Secret Weapon

Nature is one of the best weapons for fighting a down mood. When we are feeling depressed or stuck in a rut, the balance of nature helps to calm us. By simply stepping out into the grass, we can find a sense of peace otherwise lost in between walls and manufactured environments. Mother Nature has therapeutic effects on the human body. Humans crave a connection with nature that dates back to the very first humans who lived amongst lush forests, tropical gardens growing abundantly, and wild animals running free. People walked around engaging with nature, touching the leaves on the trees, walking barefoot through the grass. Man has found solace in nature for many centuries. When was the last time you spent quality time in nature? Nature is like a best friend; it will always be there, even when you aren't available. Nature will always be open to playing and spending time with you, even when it isn't convenient for you. Imagine if you treat nature with the same respect that you do a best friend. Why not make nature your new BFF?

The benefits of spending a little time outside are tremendous. For starters it gives you a natural high. Smelling the fresh morning air and feeling the cool breeze is one simple way to feel alive and fully in your body. If we started each morning with a breath of fresh air before we even checked email, brushed teeth, or ate breakfast, we would see immediate returns on this simple activity. Wake up each morning, step outside, and breathe in all of life. Listen to the birds greeting you, feel the warm sun shine down on your cheeks, balanced with the cool morning breeze. Breathe in and out for a few minutes and start your day fresh. Nature has played an integral role in the quest for happiness and personal fulfillment of many historical figures such as Ralph Waldo Emerson, John Muir, and Charles Darwin. Frank Lloyd Wright (1867-1959), architect and philosopher, advised, "Study nature, love nature, stay close to nature. It will never fail you."

Becoming one with nature can also help reduce stress. A study established that a view of nature, even through a window, speeds recovery from surgery, improves work performance, and increases job satisfaction. I once worked in an environment that had no windows. It was like a dungeon, and the turnover rate was extremely high. It is no coincidence that being closed off from the outside world will increase depression. Choose to embrace nature. Sit by a window, or set up your desk outside on the deck to breathe in fresh air. Take mini recess breaks to literally go outside and play with the earth. Nature will reward you in many ways. First, it will provide an instant upgrade of your mood to feeling more, calm, balanced, and at peace.

Being in nature also gives us a sense of connectedness, meaning, and purpose. There is a sense of chaotic order in the way nature works; the plants and animals are interconnected in a series of complex relationships. Everything coexists in nature without the necessity of outside intervention. It is a brilliant system that has existed successfully since the beginning of time, providing a sense of structure, coherence, and reliability. Realizing that human beings are an essential component of this larger structure can supply a sense of purpose and belonging.

Respect and enjoyment of nature also leads to a sense of spirituality and an appreciation for powers larger than oneself. The wilderness teaches that each individual is unique, but also part of the larger whole. In a world bogged down by social, economical and cultural pressures, standards of conduct, and the demands of others, nature gives people a chance to appreciate a grander sense that the world is alive, fascinating, and meaningful. This universal appeal crosses all cultures and time periods. If you are feeling down, just step outside into nature and see your mood switch around.

Nature Is a Teacher

Nature is one of the best teachers to help us through life. The simple balance of everything coexisting and functioning together makes it easy to recognize that there can be lessons found outdoors. Whether we look to individual aspects of nature or the entire ecosystem, we can lean on Mother Nature to teach us valuable life lessons. For instance, look at the life cycle of a tree. The process of growing from a tiny seed into a huge, leafy adult tree takes hundreds, sometimes thousands of years. What a perfect representation of patience. General Sherman, the largest tree in the world, is a fantastic example of patience. Located in Sequoia National Park, near Visalia, California, the tree is 275 feet tall and almost 52,513 cubic feet. It takes thousands of years for a tree to grow that tall. The oldest tree in the world, *Pinus Longaeva*, is believed to be 4,844 years old, which makes the tree one of the oldest growing things on earth. Imagine the amount of changes this tree has had to endure in order to stand tall today.

The same goes for humans. Each new experience brings a new outcome in our lives, but we have to learn to weather the hard times in order to stand tall and make it through to the next bright sunny day. The trees grow tall into the sky reaching their branches up towards the sunlight to allow the shadows to fall below them. When we find ourselves in a difficult situation all we have to do is turn our heads up to the bright sky and let the sunlight fall onto our faces, allowing the fears and worries to fall behind us like the shadows of the trees.

I've learned that the trick to enjoying life is to experience it fully, which means just like the tree that weathers the elements, we must learn to live through, accept, and appreciate the tough times as well as the good times. The tree endures everything from the natural weather patterns of earth to the evolution of society; a tree is a survivor and a wise source of inspiration. The power of patience is immense, especially when we want to create a fulfilling life. The saying "all good things come to those who wait" may be a cliché, but it is true. When we wait for things we want we often feel more gratitude when we receive them. We feel more abundant after waiting or working hard towards something. There are two parts to being patient. There is the waiting aspect, and then there is the most important part, the knowing part. Most people don't ever get to or understand the power of knowing, rather "trusting" the process. When we are truly patient we can afford to wait without worry because we know that the outcome will be in our favor. My mother used to always say, "It is either this or something better," meaning if the outcome of any situation didn't look like what I wanted, it would then be something even better, and it was always on its way.

Think about you life and something you really wanted, but you had to be patient for it — maybe applying for school and waiting for the acceptance letter, waiting for a second date from your future "I do," or maybe hearing back about your dream job. Whatever the life situation, trust that whatever happens will be the correct course of action. If the date never calls you back, that means someone better is right around the corner on their way to you, but if you took a date with Mr. or Ms. Wrong, then you'd be farther off course from being with the right person for you. The same goes for jobs. The dream job in your head might not be as cool as the dream job you get when you let go of the outcome and trust the process of patience. This is a difficult concept to grasp at first because we think we know what we want and what will be best for us. There are always other factors in every situation that we cannot see. Remember to trust that the universe has a plan much greater then ours.

For example, a few years ago, I had a job interview at what I thought was my dream company. I felt like I nailed the interview and I was a total shoo-in. A few weeks later, I found they had filled the position with another person. Naturally, I felt bummed, but only for a moment as I picked myself up and said, "Okay what's next? It is this or something better. Just because I thought that was my perfect fit, doesn't mean that there isn't something else out there that is better suited for me." And there was. I ended up landing a better job with a company that fit my personality better. So I was able to go to work and express myself and work with like-minded people, without having to conform to a corporate stale environment. This happens all of the time in life when we think our outcome must be one way in order for us to be happy. I have coached clients who have been desperate for specific outcomes, only to find when they don't get what they wanted they crumble to the floor in tears of rage. I know how hard it is. I used to live my life like that, too, until I discovered the real power of patience.

Awesome Opportunity:

1. The first step is to declare what you want. Write down your intention and take steps to work towards it.
2. When things don't happen according to your timeline, don't give up. Write down steps you can take to move back toward your goal. This is the most valuable aspect of patience.

It is human nature to want things, but in order to live a purposeful and powerful life, we must learn to relax into outcomes and trust that things will always work in our favor. *A Course in Miracles* states, "Those who are certain of the outcome can afford to wait, and wait without anxiety." Think about our friend the tree. He grows tall, patient, and wise. He does not worry about the outcome or fear the unknown; he simply coexists with his surroundings. The grass, the dirt, the birds, and squirrels all help make his home comfortable. The same goes for us if we want something to happen in our lives. Rather than trying to force it or manipulate time, people, or energy, to make it happen on our timeline, we can relax into the flow of life, and let "nature take its course."

Many people are not aware that they can control their surroundings by practicing patience and peace from within. Learning to appreciate the moment is a good first step. The same way a child makes a mud pie or catches fireflies in the yard, an adult can learn to be in the moment and become closer to nature. When we trust that everything is in right order, and that whatever outcome prevails will be the right outcome, we can trust the process of patience. Having patience is one of the easiest steps to loving your life to the fullest. When we relax into the rhythm of life, we can flow with its currents rather than fight up stream like a salmon.

Nature for Good Health

"There is nothing more satisfying than eating right! The domino effect that occurs will influence every nook and cranny of your life." — Kris Carr

It's no secret that choosing natural, organic foods grown from the earth will give you great health. In general, when we eat more fruits and vegetables rather than processed sugary, carb-injected, fake food we feel better, our insides function better and we have more energy. The domino effect of eating healthy food is tremendous. When I start my morning with fresh lemon water or tea, I feel five times better than when I start with a latte loaded with cream and sugar. Naturally, my lunch is healthier; I usually choose better snacks and even have a better workout each day. However, when I wake up and go straight to sugar and processed junk food, refined carbs or sugar-loaded cereal my body has to work overtime just to digest and process all the foreign food. While my body is spending time trying to process all the sugary food, it is using energy that could have been used to enjoy my day and help me fulfill my dreams. When my body is trying to digest such foreign foods it takes a lot of energy, and I feel tired more quickly.

I have tried many diets to find what works best for me. I tried a paleo diet, which is to eat only what our ancestors ate, vegetarian (no meat), vegan (no animal products), raw, only natural uncooked foods, Atkins, meat and lots of meat . . . and the list goes on. I have arrived at a place where no diet is best, and listening to my body is my diet. When I ate ice cream, I noticed how my taste buds loved it, but my digestive track was uncomfortable, so I limited my dairy and saw my face clear up instantly. I noticed that when I ate meat I didn't digest the food for a few days, but when I ate lots of healthy, leafy greens, tofu and polenta, I felt like a million bucks. Bottom line is, do what feels right for yourself, however there is no denying that eating foods from nature will give you more energy, power and help you look, feel and be your best. Maybe try it out for a few weeks. What do you have to lose? Just look at your eating habits and see how you are feeling. See what the connection is between the two and maybe switch up some small habits. See if you can trade in coffee for tea two days a week, or choose an apple instead of baked chips. Think natural and organic, and choose wisely.

There is a trick to grocery shopping. Only shop on the outside perimeter, where you will find the fresh produce and natural foods. Generally items on the inside are processed, refined and loaded with chemicals and sugar. I also shop at farmer's markets. Buying locally is a great way to reduce your carbon footprint and help the community. When you do that, you naturally feel better about yourself, and thus turning any down mood into a happy one.

Nature and Your Magic List

Becoming best friends with nature is easy when you start to see the benefits of playing in it, eating it and loving it daily. When it comes to loving life fully, including nature is a must. Adding things to do in nature to your magic list is a great way to love life. Whether it is growing a garden, learning to surf, hiking up a volcano, volunteering as a camp counselor or climbing K2 Mountain, involving nature in your magic list will help make life more fulfilling.

In a Nutshell:

1. Spending time in nature reduces stress and can help maintain balance.
2. Nature can teach us lessons about patience, coexisting, balance, and order.
3. Your body will thank you for eating natural, organic foods.
4. Adding things to do in nature to your magic list will help you feel more alive.

Additional Resources:

Audio Meditation: *Find Your Happy: Motivational Mantras,* Track 11, "Practice Patience" (available on iTunes, amazon.com, and playwiththeworld.com shop).

CHAPTER FIFTEEN

DANCE LIKE NO ONE IS WATCHING

*"Why compare yourself with others? No one in the entire world can do a better job of being you than you." — **Unknown***

The Art of Being You

There is only one you in the entire world. No one else will ever be able to do exactly what you do in the way you do it, so at this point in our journey it is necessary to understand how awesome you truly are. No one in the world has your experience, your knowledge, your thought patterns, your history, family and friends. What you bring to each situation impacts the rest of the world. When you are not there the energy is different. Whether you skip a chance to spend time with friends or call in sick to work, when you are absent you are missed. So appreciate yourself and the contributions that you have to give this world.

I spent the majority of my life trying to be someone I wasn't. I didn't even know that I was being inauthentic to me. Because the rest of society was busy graduating from school, getting good jobs, getting married, and landing big promotions, I just assumed that's what we all needed to do. It took me years to figure out that perhaps there was a better way for me to live my life. And it started because I got clear with myself about what I really wanted out of my life.

It took a major life stressor to show me the possibilities for living passionately and honestly. For the first time in my life, I was forced to ask, "What do I really want?" Rather than just going with the flow, I was excited to learn that my passion for travel and writing was more than just a tiny dream; it could be a real and fulfilling career. So I spent time learning more about myself, discovering what I really wanted and pulled out the magic list. I started to tackle that bad boy and published many stories in travel magazines and inspirational books, such as *Chicken Soup for the Soul*. This led me to create the website *playwiththeworld.com*, a site dedicated to helping others find true happiness and purpose in their lives through adventure, travel, articles, lectures and inspirational mantras. This is who I am. Who are you?

Most of us spend our entire life walking around half dead, just going through the motions and trying to make do with what life hands us. It takes a truly dedicated person to see opportunities in every aspect of life. Real happiness is making the most out of the good times and the bad times. Real, lasting, and fulfilling joy comes from embracing life and your role in it. When you step into your power and your true authentic self, you shine. You shine so brightly that the world tries to keep up. Opportunities fly at you from every angle. It starts with asking yourself one thing, "What do I want?" After asking yourself what you really want, you will quickly be able to determine who you are. Who are you? You are uniquely you, and you are here to do one special thing that no one else in the world can do, because they are not you. Many times we stop ourselves from following through on dreams because we think, "It's been done," or "No one really cares if I say or do this." But this is our doubter kicking us in the pants.

Rule number one for mastering a manifesting life is to kick the doubter to the curb. When it says mean things, punch it back with positive comments. For every negative comment, say three positive ones. For example, maybe you have a goal of learning a new language but your doubter comes in and says, "You aren't even going to the country anytime soon. You will never use that language; it is dumb and a waste of time." Your job is to recognize this voice as just a cover, not part of you. It is not you saying this, just that little mean monster on your left shoulder. Gently say, "I hear you, but I have always wanted to learn

French, and Paris is one of the most beautiful cities in the world. I will go one day, and I will be more fulfilled knowing that I am bilingual. Plus it will look great on my resume."

See what we did? Boom! Boom! Pow! We sucker punched that negative nastiness right back to No-Go-Ville. Next time you want to try to make something happen, first recognize that you do matter and the fact that you had the inspiration come into your head means it is worth pursuing. Cast your fishing line out and start catching big dreams. You do matter and you are fabulous just the way you are.

Shake What Your Mama Gave You

The same way that you are uniquely you and no one else in the world can do what you do, no one else in the world looks just like you. In fact, no two people in the world have the same body shape in the exact proportions. It took me a long time to realize this. I used to compare myself to other people and wonder why my thighs were always bigger. It wasn't until I realized that the same little voice that keeps us from following through on our dreams was the same little nasty thing that was telling me horrible things about myself. I couldn't look in the mirror and see anything good. This contributed to the depression and the addictions. I was just stuck in a big vicious cycle.

When we let little nasty into our thoughts, little nasty can do some damaging things. The same way we are what we eat, we are what we think. I would tell myself I wasn't good enough, that I didn't get the job because I was too overweight or underweight or whatever stage I was in that that particular moment. I would belittle myself and say such horrible things that it made it impossible to love myself or even give anyone else real lasting love. In order to get love, you have to give it. No matter how much someone else loves you or you love other people, if you don't love yourself then it can never be enough. In order to really take off and embrace every aspect of your life you must start with you, which means loving what your mama gave you. Thick thighs, thin hair, blotchy skin — whatever it is that has you hung up — let it go and know that you are awesome because no one else in the world looks like you.

Do you think animals go around comparing themselves to one another? Does a squirrel go up to another squirrel and say, "Dang it, your tail is longer than mine! My hands are smaller than yours. I suck so much because I can't get as many nuts as you"? No they don't. Humans are the only animal that manifests negative thought patterns of comparison and self-ridicule. Recognizing that it doesn't do us any good can be the first step to releasing it. Just let go of comparisons and any outcome connected to how you look.

Once I recognized that I was a victim of my own negative nasty thoughts, I quickly switched gears. I started to say kind things to myself. I would smile and thank the universe for my healthy body. I would hold gratitude for all of the athletic, adventurous things my healthy body lets me do. Slowly, I started to let go of the negative perceptions. By saying kind things to yourself and loving yourself for who you are you will feel more free and joyous in life. It is a beautiful feeling when you finally do accept yourself for who you are. It took me many years and many hours of conscious thinking to arrive at a place of self-satisfaction but I can tell you now that I am here, it is beautiful to no longer be consumed by calorie counting, obsessing over workouts or dreading my next wardrobe reinvention. I am happy with me. Being happy with everything about yourself is one key part of *Find Your Happy*. Bring your happy back by loving yourself fully.

Awesome Opportunity:

Here are some simple things to do right now to get you on the right path to self-love.

1. Recognize that you are you, uniquely you, and no one else can do, be, or look like you.
2. Write down your strengths. What are you good at? What do you like to do?
3. Recognize that you make a difference.
4. What is something nice that someone has said to you lately? Write out something nice to say about you. Make a mini list of attributes and positive qualities that are true about you. Write it down and read it every morning.

5. When the negative nasty comes in, squash it with positive loving. What is something your negative nasty has said lately? Now respond back with three positive truths. Squash that little bugger.

Shine Your Light

What happens when you accept yourself for who you are and follow your heart to discover your true purpose? Your inner light can shine through. You are able to be true to yourself and represent a place of integrity, honor and admiration. People will want to be around you all the time. You will be the person in the room that people cannot take their eyes away from. People will say they want what you have and it is all because you are being the real, honest, authentic you. Ask yourself if you are currently in love with every aspect of your life. At this point in your *Find Your Happy* journey, you should be getting pretty close because the real magic of being happy in life is learning and accepting the good times and the bad.

When we are in times of trouble, we reach out to loved ones, to the universe, and to our inner self. When we reach within and count on our wisdom, experience, courage, and ability to choose positive thoughts, then we find ourselves in a sense of peace, a joy that floods throughout every aspect of our lives. Recognize that the universe is working with you to make your life even more awesome than you could possibly imagine. We all have an inner light that wants to shine brightly. Letting the real you come out and play is a magical experience. Your light will shine so brightly that the rest of the world will need shades. You will be the cool friends' cooler friend.

Life happens and it is up to us to make the most out of it. We will begin to see life open up and opportunities fly into our daily routines when we ask ourselves the real questions: Who am I? Who do I want to be? How can I help others? It all starts with being thankful for what you do have, loving you for yourself and what you do have to offer, and then taking the steps to offer your services to the world.

Awesome Opportunity:

1. Make a list of things you love to do.
2. Challenge yourself to make sure you do something off your list everyday.
3. A simple equation to help you get to happy:
   Do what you love everyday = happy you.

Do What Makes You Happy

Another simple trick to staying happy is to do what you love, and do it every day. When we do something we love, we are usually good at it. When we do what we are good at, we feel useful. When we feel useful, we feel validated. You see where this leads . . . abundant happiness and pure joy. Life is a giant roller coaster, but doing what we love to do as much as possible will make it easier to handle the uphill and fast downhill transitions. What you love may change from day to day, week to week or year to year, but that is okay. Trusting and understanding that we are always changing and evolving as people is part of the process.

For instance, a couple years ago I was really into endurance sports. I ran half marathons, competed in half ironman triathlons and rode century (100 mile) bike races every weekend. The process of training for such grueling events was rewarding to me, so I trained every day. I found immense happiness in participating in these events. Setting a goal, working towards it, pushing my body to extremes, and then competing with thousands of other crazy athletes and getting a new medal at the end of each race were all parts of the fulfillment. Then one day, it wasn't fun anymore. It became a chore, and I resisted it. At first, I tried to overcome my resistance. I was so confused about why something I loved so much was all of a sudden so hard to do. Then I recognized that it was part of my journey, a phase. That chapter of my life was just that, a chapter.

The current chapter that I am in still involves eating and being healthy, but not training for any event. I experienced those things and they helped pull me out of a depression. For now, I have to be okay with that being in my past and stop trying to make it my present. For awhile,

I kept signing up for events, not training for them and then missing the event. I was trying to be someone I no longer was or no longer could be. I outgrew that stage of my life. There is no telling when and if this love for endurance sports will return, but I recognize and appreciate that it had its place and time in my life.

The same thing applies to relationships and living circumstances. Not all relationships are meant to last. Each person, job, home, etc. that comes into our lives is there to help us, enlighten us and fulfill us at that particular moment. But we change. With every new person we meet and interact with, we also evolve. With every new experience we go through, we change. People don't ever really leave us, their roles just change. Change is good, and learning to be okay with change is part of shining your true authentic light. So ask yourself if you are holding onto anything too tightly. Perhaps there is an older habit that you used to have that you wish you still did; like running, baking or spending time with your family. Maybe you are ready to release habits and patterns that no longer serve you. Is it time to say "when?" When your heart feels trapped, then it is time to say "when." Maybe a relationship no longer serves you. If true, it is time to let go. Holding onto something that we used to like is one of the reasons we get depressed. Shifting our awareness to recognize that life has many chapters, and each chapter of our story evolves and helps us grow is a simple way to accept the losses. Buddha said, "Those who are free of resentful thoughts surely find peace." Learning to let go of past versions of yourself and focus on the present is one step to enlightenment and living a purposeful, conscious, happy, peaceful life.

The Sky Is Not the Limit When There Are Footprints on the Moon

When Thomas Edison was interviewed by a young reporter who boldly asked Mr. Edison if he felt like a failure and if he thought he should just give up by now. Perplexed, Edison replied, "Young man, why would I feel like a failure? And why would I ever give up? I now know definitively over 9,000 ways that an electric light bulb will not work. Success is almost in my grasp." And shortly after that, and over 10,000 attempts, Edison invented the light bulb. Thomas Edison didn't look at his current reality and accept it for what it was. Living by candlelight was all anyone had ever known until his brain had an idea, a "what if?" moment. Wondering if there was a better to create the light bulb. Using electricity for light became the normal way to live life and candlelight was a thing of the past. The same goes for any other monumental shift in history, whether it is Madonna, moving to New York with $20 in her pocket to pursue her dream to become a pop star entertainer or Barack Obama campaigning to be the first African American president in America. No progress in the world is made without people moving on their inklings. All major advances in society started with one person saying to themselves, "There has got to be a better way."

From man walking on the moon to a black man in the south declaring "I have a dream," life moves forward with people who challenge the current reality. These types of people are game changers. They look at what is, and say, "I think I can do better." They do not settle or throw their hands up in the air and give up; they challenge the current state by putting their idea into action. Authors who publish books, songwriters who perform their own music, politicians who get elected, chefs who own their own restaurants — all of these people have a few things in common: persistence, patience, and an ability to listen to their heart and question the status quo. Think for a moment about your favorite artist or your favorite musician. Maybe you have seen them play in concert. When they first step on stage, think about how you feel.

When I watch my favorite performers, something takes over. I see it in them; they became almost transcendent as they dance around on stage singing magnificent lyrics. I am so inspired that I am often moved to tears. It is in these moments that I feel connected to them, as I recognize in them what I want for myself: to be doing what I am put on earth to do. Everyone is created for something so unique that only they can do it.

The band U2, for example, has had a 30+ year career moving people around the world with their soulful music. As they do what they are naturally so gifted at, they give back to millions by inspiring fans through their soulful music and uplifting vocals. What about the band Maroon 5? Same dream to be famous musicians but a completely different vocal ensemble, often attracting different types of fans. If you have a dream to become something that you currently are not, like a famous book author, or a public speaker, or maybe you want to go back to school, travel overseas to be a teacher, whatever your dream is, do not let other things get in your way. It will be easy for the nasty little voice to creep in and say, "Your book topic has already been written about." "No one wants to pay to hear you talk." "There are already too many teachers out of work." Kick that little voice away. Imagine if Bono from the band U2 said, "Oh, there is already too much music out there, and all the songs about love and hope have already been written." U2 is so unique with their personal twists that no one in the world can even compare. The same goes for you, my dear. Whatever it is that you want to do, be, and have is yours when you allow yourself to believe in the dream. No one can do it like you. Don't shoot for the moon, because there are planets far beyond that. I always say if you are going to aim for the moon aim higher.

I once heard about a women who had a dream to visit every country in the world before she dies. This averaged out to seven countries a year, for 30 years. Her husband thought she was crazy, and society certainly didn't look upon a dream like that with bright eyes. She believed in her dream so much that she challenged the status quo. Rather than taking a trip a year, like most people long to, she went big, and said, "I will travel to at least seven countries every year." By doing so, she created her career as a traveler, a consultant and a writer describing her travels. She volunteered in Russia at a children's school, and was able to make her dream a reality with enough persistence, passion and patience. Think about what you really want in life, and then go even bigger. Challenge yourself to think larger than life and then let go of the outcome. Trust that your dream is on its way to you because when we lead our lives with our hearts we can accomplish tremendous things. The life you've always wanted is on its way to you when you give it permission to breathe.

In a Nutshell:

1. Appreciate yourself and the contributions that you have to give this world.

2. Real happiness is making the most of the good times and the bad times.

3. Recognize the fear voice and quickly cover it up with three positive affirmations.

4. You do matter and you are fabulous just the way you are.

5. Humans are the only animal that manifests the negative thought patterns of comparison and self-ridicule. Think more like an animal and be in a state of flow.

6. Answer the questions: Who am I? What do I want? How can I help others?

7. Do what you love every day.

8. Always ask, "What if?"

9. Whatever the dream is, dream bigger.

Additional Resources:

Audio Meditation: *Find Your Happy: Motivational Mantras*, Track 7, "Perfect Just the Way You Are" (available on iTunes, amazon.com, and playwiththeworld.com shop).

CHAPTER SIXTEEN

MAKE THE IMPOSSIBLE POSSIBLE

*"To get something you never had, you have to
do something you never did." — Unknown*

Live Outside of Your Comfort Zone

I always liked the idea of chasing rainbows and making the impossible possible. Some people would argue that the idea of chasing rainbows has the connotation of trying really hard and never getting anywhere. There is the adage about never being able to find the pot of gold at the end of the rainbow, so it feels and seems like an impossible task. But what if the impossible is really possible? The word possible is part of impossible. In fact the word is spelled "I'm • Possible." Naturally our brains are conditioned to think that some things are too hard or too much work, but the very nature of impossible tasks is to push through, challenge, and evolve past the boundaries in order to literally make the impossible possible. Looking at it this way, chasing rainbows is fun and an exciting challenge. In reality, we push through fears and challenges that seem too hard, we grow, and we gain strength, courage, understanding, and wisdom.

Everybody has a comfort zone and that comfort zone is different for each person. Only you know what your comfort level is, but pushing that level is a gorgeous opportunity to find lasting happiness. When you are constantly evolving as a person, pushing through your own fear and trying new things, you naturally settle into the rhythm of life and love it fully. Whether pushing your comfort zone is trying a new career, trying something new like cooking, or diving into a relationship that is new, life will always present opportunities for us to try something new. When we try something new, we can then decide if we like it or not.

I coached a client who proclaimed how much he hated sushi. The thought of eating raw fish freaked him out but his new girlfriend really loved it. He refused to give into the notion of shoveling slimy scales into his mouth. I asked him if he had ever tried sushi, and he replied, "No." The problem was obvious. He was so settled in his comfort zone that he was unwilling to try something new. I asked him what would happen if he tried sushi, would he die? I mean really what is the worst that would happen? Maybe he would spit it out because it tasted bad. My point was, "How would you ever know if you don't try it?" He followed my advice and took his girlfriend to a surprise sushi date and he totally surprised himself. He learned that not all sushi is raw fish. To his dismay, he actually enjoyed it. Seeing how much his significant other enjoyed it increased his enjoyment, and now they have regular sushi dates.

Awesome Opportunity:

1. What do you refuse to do because it is out of your comfort zone? Maybe you refuse to speak in front of an audience, buy a big-ticket item, or ask that cute barista out, because it is outside of your comfort zone? Make a list of things that you resist because they are uncomfortable.
2. Ask yourself what is on the other side of that experience, such as personal freedom, self-expression, or more peace.
3. What is the worst that will happen if you do it?
4. If you are okay with the outcome, then schedule a time to do it.

By practicing pushing through your comfort zone, your world will open up. You will experience new things and begin to see a longer horizon. Life will naturally feel more fulfilling.

What if the worst thing that "could" happen is death? Take, for example, skydiving. This activity was on my magic list and I asked myself, "What is it about this activity that is so exciting?" It was the thrill of free falling, pushing my fears aside and literally busting through the comfort zone of feeling comfortable, cozy, and secure on the ground. What is on the other side of this activity? It was the thrill of living, feeling and embracing life. What could happen if it went wrong? Well, I could die. I had to check in and make sure that I would have been okay with that outcome. I certainly don't have a death wish, but when you live life to the fullest and love every moment, there are no regrets so dying becomes part of life. You can accept it without throwing all caution to the wind and being silly. I had to say to myself, "Well if I die, then it will be while I am doing something I love." I choose to live life fully and that means taking calculated risks and busting through fears to live a purposeful, powerful life.

Take Risks, Be a Gutsy Guru

Taking risks is common when you embrace life and settle in to true happiness. Enjoying each moment is no longer risky, but a chance to try new things. At this point in your journey you will recognize the benefits of taking risks, ranging from relieving stress and growing as a person, to opening yourself up to meeting people who can help you reach your goals.

It takes guts to conjure up the courage to do things on the other side of fear. But every time we bust through it, we feel enlightened, happy and more fulfilled. If you find yourself still feeling a little stuck in trying to reach your goals, then think about your ultimate outcome. What do you want and why do you want it? The reason "why" should be the focus that pulls you through the fear. Only hold space for the feelings of happiness that come with accomplishing your goal.

One of my good friends set out three years ago to do something that had never been done before. He looked at the way things were, and said to himself, "This isn't the best way. I can do better." Just like Michelangelo, Oprah or the Beatles, he trusted his gut and followed though with action. He set out to change the way people exchange money. He would go out with friends to eat or do business transitions and notice that when exchanging money, it took a few days to get the funds from one hand from the other. He had a vision of instant transferring, faster than PayPal, faster and more convenient than anything that had ever been created before. He left his job to dive into his dream completely. He took a giant risk, leaving everything he knew, but he trusted his heart and pushed towards what he thought was a better way. For him the vision, feeling, and goal of helping others make online banking faster, more convenient, and easier to use was his guiding power. What is your guiding power? If you want to lose 15 pounds, hold the vision of a vibrant, healthy you in your mind. Focus on what you want. Feel the feelings associated with what you want. Whatever it is you want, focus on it until you get it.

My friend worked day in and day out, and now the product is in the marketplace. He is a millionaire and has literally changed the way money transfers can occur. His company is the way of the future. It took one man with an idea, a vision, and putting action behind it, then believing in it so intently that he gave his dream everything he had. This is courage; this takes guts.

Being a gutsy guru means taking chances, like my friend, going against the grain to do what feels right for you. To be truly happy we must let go of what others think is best for us. If my friend listened to every doubter along the way, he would not have changed the face of banking for the better. If he doubted himself and refused to listen to his gut then he would not be a millionaire. Ask yourself if doubters are keeping you from what you want. What are the external sources? What internal dialog is playing? Recognize them and release them to the universe. The doubter does not belong in the gutsy equation. Being a gutsy guru also means taking chances and trusting yourself. Every single person has an intuition, a gut feeling, that guides us to happiness. When we hone in on this feeling, we can experience abundant happiness and real lasting joy. Listening to your gut is as simple as learning to trust yourself.

The human intuition is the guiding power that protects us from harm and keeps us on course. Have you ever felt a certain way, maybe nervous or anxious, about a situation and it caused you to take a different route, and then afterwards you found that that route was indeed the right one? This is the intuition at work. It will always guide us in the direction we need to go. When we ignore it, our feelings of anxiety, rage, fear, and depression take over. I sat in a deep depression for so many years because I refused to listen to my intuition. It kept saying, "This isn't right. Don't do this. This doesn't fit who you are," but I ignored it, all in an effort to find my happiness. When I stopped to listen to that intuition, it turned out my happiness was inside. Listening to our intuitive voice will always take us to happiness. In order to access a constant state of happiness and flow we must trust our internal guidance system.

Master Fear

Fear is not a bad thing; it actually helps us know when we are getting close to greatness. Fear is connected to the ego and the ego wants to protect us. The left-brain rational mind, often called the ego, is that little nasty that keeps us from trying new experiences, doing new things and spending time with new people. Learning to recognize it as a friend on our journey to happiness is one more step to happiness. When we let go of fear and its ability to control our thoughts, we can balance out our lives. Fear is just an indicator, and after a bit of calling it out, it begins to get smaller. Once we recognize it as fear and not as us it becomes much smaller and more approachable. So call out your fear. What is it and why is there?

We have done quite a bit of work up to this point to release fears, but it is important to take it one step further and tackle them for good. Remember, earlier we asked ourselves what believing in our fear cost? Usually it keeps us from what we want. Then we asked why we believe this fear. Usually something happened a long time ago, and the ego stepped in and said, "I don't ever want that to happen again," so it caused us to avoid the situation. Maybe you fear speaking in front of a crowd and you realize that when you were seven, in show and tell, you dropped your toy, and the entire class laughed at you. You felt embarrassed and separated from the rest of the class. Since then you have hated getting up in front of a group. Explore your fears and try to get in touch with their source. The next, and final step, is to recognize the reality of the situation, the real truth of your fear. That fear is fake, and not real. To master your fear is as simple as reminding yourself what is the truth.

Fear shows up in many ways. Notice how it shows up and how you act. As I mentioned, fear used to paralyze me. I literally froze up and couldn't move forward. I cried a lot because I knew what was on the other side of my fear was happiness. It wasn't until I sat with this feeling and recognized that fear was just an indicator that I was getting close to the unknown. I was scooting outside my comfort zone. I busted through it. Real happiness exists on the other side of fear. Take off into the new you by looking at your fears, challenging them and busting through. It is always better on the other side.

Continuous Effort = Unlocked Potential

People who urge you to be realistic generally want you to accept their version of reality, which is often limited. When you learn to embrace the *Play with the World* mentality, life becomes full of opportunities and when you set your mind to something, it will come true. People around you may have a hard time keeping up, but the people who stay close to your side are your real friends. Those who cast judgment are usually the type of people who are afraid of change and fear the unknown. They are not the people who will be game changers, inventors or even people who follow their own heart. You have big dreams and a lot to do and see in this life, so when you do set you mind on a goal the last and final step is to put continuous effort towards achieving it.

A lot of law of attraction books and self-help mavens suggest that if you think about it, it will come. In her book, *The Secret,* Rhonda Byrne made this notion available to the masses. Think about what you want, feel it and you will attract it. This is partially true. This does work, but the part that most people get frustrated with is that it doesn't always come true when they think it should. Part of manifesting and making the most out of your life is to continue to put effort towards what you want, even when you don't necessarily "see" it becoming a reality. Don't ever give up.

Take, for example, my goal to become a travel writer. Even though I was in corporate, stuck behind a desk, I looked at postcards I had placed on my cubicle wall from cities around the world that I longed to visit. This was the first step. To declare what I wanted and visualize it, I used a vision board. I started to write and pursue this dream. I acted as if it was already a reality. Even though I was going to an office each day, I would daydream about the places I would write about in the future. It provided my heart with such satisfaction that it became natural for me to start to see it as a reality. The more I thought about it, the more people I met who were connected with the publishing world. Best-selling authors soon became my good friends, mentors, and coaches. Publishers of national magazines were starting to talk to me about the potential of working together. I continued to write and submit articles to magazines. The more I wrote, the more I was published. I pushed forward with my dream, putting continuous action into what I wanted and it started to manifest into my reality.

The next part is critical and the part that people most often fail to do, therefore their dreams often do not become a reality. They forget to let go . . . literally let go of the expectation of when and how your dream will become true. When I was focusing on becoming a full-time writer I learned how important it was to trust the process. The things I learned prepared me for where I am right now. At that time, if someone had handed me a golden ticket and said, "Okay, you are a travel writer," I would have fallen flat on my face, because I had to yet to build a bridge to my goal.

The work we do between where we are now and where we want to be is manifested because of the experiences we have, we have people we meet, and the knowledge we gain. A bridge must be set in place to get from here to there. Trusting that you are doing everything right and that things will fall into to place is the final aspect of making your dreams a golden opportunity. If I had thrown in the towel on my dream because things weren't happening as fast as I wanted, or they didn't look the way I wanted them to, then my dream would have never come true. When we have goals and dreams it takes time to make them a reality, but when we believe in them, when we trust that they will come true, and when we know that everything is working in perfect order to help us achieve them, we will become true happiness gurus. That way when we want something we know it will happen. When, where, and how doesn't matter because we know that the specific outcome we want with each dream, will come true if and when it is in our higher best interest.

You may think you want something but if it doesn't happen the way you expected, ask yourself why. Usually it is because you thought of the outcome and how great it would be. But what if the outcome is always better than we imagine? When we trust that our dreams will come true, and we put actions towards them, they can manifest much faster.

However, there is a fine line between pushing and pulling. Our dreams can only come to manifestation when we are in a state of flow. If we are manipulating or trying to grasp and make things happen, then we restrict the flow. Often our dreams will come to a screeching stop, because we are trying to literally play "God." We try to make things happen the way we want, when we want, the natural process of dreams cannot occur. It gets restricted. Ask yourself if you are holding on to anything too intently. If so, release the constraints a little and let the process happen. Watch what miracles can occur when you let the people who are supposed to come to you come. When you trust the process, happiness can flow.

Awesome Opportunity:

1. Declare what you want.
2. Visualize it by creating a vision board.
3. Put action towards it.
4. Keep putting actions towards it.
5. Remember to let it flow. Let go of outcomes and timelines.
6. Watch awesomeness flood your way.

In a Nutshell:

1. When busting through fear ask what is the worst that can happen?
2. Every time you bust through fear, you will feel enlightened, happy, and more fulfilled.
3. Trust your gut and follow through with your actions.
4. Focus on what you want. Feel the feelings associated with what you want. Don't give up on the dream. It will come true, always.

5. Listening to our intuitive voice will always take us to happiness.
6. Fear is not a bad thing; it actually helps us know when we are getting close to greatness.
7. When you set your mind to something, it will come true.
8. Let go of the expectation of when and how your dream will become true in order to make it come true.

Additional Resources:

Audio Meditation: *Find Your Happy: Motivational Mantras,* Track 13, "Don't Give Up" (available on iTunes, amazon.com, and playwiththeworld.com shop).

CHAPTER SEVENTEEN

HUG YOUR INNER CHILD

"You know you're in love when you can't fall asleep because reality is finally better than your dreams." — *Dr. Seuss*

Say Hello to Mini You

You are perfect, precious, and awesome just as you are. When you were a child, you did not judge, analyze or beat yourself up for making a mistake. You simply were. You were a perfect being, comfortable in your own skin, and happy to be alive. Unfortunately, things happen in life that bring us down. People come into our lives and hurt us and we learn to not trust others. The real beauty in life is to recognize that none of these experiences define who we are. If classmates made fun of us in middle school for being stupid or fat, and we grow up relating to the world as a stupid or fat person, then we are doing a disservice to ourselves and the rest of the world. Our mission is to get in touch with the mini mes of the world. Find your mini you and hug it dearly. Your mini you wants to be heard, your mini you does have an opinion, and it is almost always to choose love and play. Play is one way to access more happiness in your life. Learning to play and make the most out of your day is as important as everything else we have discussed. When you are in constant connection with your mini you, play is a priority.

Adults get so burdened with responsibilities, but even responsibilities can become fun. Learn to look at everything as an opportunity to choose playtime over chore time. How can you turn your chores into a game? Life is a big game, and now you are playing it. Access mini you and ask it daily, "What do you want to do? Where do you want to go? Who do you want to talk to?"

Trust your mini you because it will always guide you to happiness. When we deny it attention, it will act out, the same as when you deny a child love and support. It will turn away and create a diversion in an effort to find happiness. If mini you isn't being cared for, it will sink into a depression. Our inner voice, our inner child, and intuition are all one. How do you know when you are listening to mini you? Well, when it feels right, that is mini you, your inner child (your heart) speaking. If it feels like a chore, a burden, or a responsibility then that is the adult you. There is a way to allow both to coexist together. Honing in on what your mini you really wants is the access point to loving every single second of every day. Suddenly, paying bills is fun, or unloading the dishwasher is all part of embracing life. Just as a child has fun playing in the mud, your adult you will be joined at the hip with mini you and life will feel rewarding. Trust yourself and trust that mini you is ready to come out and play.

Imagination Is Power

How do you access mini you? For starters, tap into your imagination. Doctor Seuss was a king of imagination. He was a man who pushed the envelope of creativity. His life was controlled by his imagination and he was very much in touch with his mini him. When you were younger did you have an imaginary friend? Why not have an adult imaginary friend, your inner guide and intuition, otherwise recognized as mini you? Your mini you has an imagination, unlike any other and it so wants to come out and play. Imagination is the number one aspect of *Play with the World* and the reason that dreams can come true. We have to think it to achieve it. If we didn't have an imagination we could not have goals or dreams. So get in touch with yours and let it play. Let it dance around and touch all of the wonderful things that life has to offer. Your imagination is part of you. Love it, hold it, care for it and let it grow. The more imagination you use, the more of your dreams can come true. The more imaginative you are, the faster your dreams can come alive.

When You Grow Up, Be a Kid Again

What did you want to be when you were a child? Are you that astronaut, that zookeeper, that designer? If not, what happened? Why did you decide to do what you are doing now? If part of you still dreams about being what you could have been, then consider reinventing yourself. If you were doing what you wanted to do, you would be living your bliss. Why are you holding yourself back from being happy?

Life has a funny way of rewarding us when we follow our hearts. Listening to your gut and mini you will get you to true, abundant happiness. Let life flow. Now that you are an adult, you can be a kid again. Go to the playground and have fun with nature. Enjoy playing outside. Parents often say that after having their first child they have learned to lighten up and laugh more. Being around children opens up a part of us that gets closed off over the years. Children laugh, love, and get excited about almost everything. When you spend time with them, they help you recognize the real things that are important in life. Learning to love your inner child is important. When we accept our inner child, we feel more balanced and life seems more grandiose. Everything becomes a thing of awe and beauty. Things are interesting and intriguing. We become curious and excited about life. Little things are more exciting than big things, and life's special moments are celebrated every second.

Life Is One Big Recess

Oh my goodness! Let out a huge big sigh and throw your hands in the air. It is recess time! Life is a big recess when you are happy, and finding your happiness is natural when you listen to yourself and your inner child. Think about recess when we were children. It was a time of play, a time of laughter, recreation, and fun. It was outside and always spent with friends. When we embrace the *Play with the World* life we live in one giant big recess. We slide through life and embrace the happy moments and the disturbing ones. Just like swinging on the swing set, life will go up and down, but when we are on recess it is always fun.

Get Your Fun On

"We don't stop playing because we grow old;

we grow old because we stop playing." — George Bernard Shaw

This quote seems to resonate with many adults. Fun is the final aspect of making the most out of your life. Imagine living every moment in a fun zone. Fun emanates from your pores and you have a perma grin as you walk through life. This vision isn't so far from the truth when you discover your happy and hug it every day. Making time for fun is a thing of the past. When you embrace the *Play with the World* life, scheduling a vacation and planning things to look forward to are no longer necessary because your life is one big vacation. Sure, you work, but the work you do is rewarding and feels like fun, and the time it takes to do anything is no longer a chore because life is fun.

To get there from here, you start by adding more fun into your daily routine. Immediately start to look at your current environment and ask yourself, "What can I do to add more fun into this scene?" If you are sitting at a desk, maybe add some fun colors, repaint a bedroom wall, change out pictures, put a funny hat on and smile more. Take little steps to activate your mini you and play with the world more. When we stop taking life so seriously and remove anger and frustration from our daily routine, fun and play can come out and shine. Visit a playground or get out some crayons and start to doodle. One of my favorites is to pull out sidewalk chalk. Nothing screams childhood more than coloring on things you are not supposed to. Pick bright colors, and just let your imagination go. Play more for a daily dose of fun. When we play often, we grow younger. In fact, by adding a daily dose of play we can grow younger every day.

In our culture many people worry about getting older. What if I told you I have a cure for aging? The perfect anti-aging regimen is play. Call me crazy, but age is nothing but a number. Wrinkles, gray hair, and age spots add wisdom and character.

For example, meet Joan, my Grandma. She is over 90 years old, loves to laugh and play, and she still shakes her groove thing on the dance floor at every family wedding. I know another grandma, not mine, who is 70 and she can't move nearly as well. She has had plastic surgery and her body aches all the time. She does not get on the dance floor. Would you rather hang out with a natural 90-year-old who is rocking it out and shaking her groove thing on the dance floor at a wedding, or sit down with a botox-injected 70-year-old wallflower? My point is that natural is more beautiful, and it will keep you dancing longer. My grandma's secret weapon for enjoying every moment of life is laughter and play. She plays every day, whether she reads a new book and lets her imagination run away with the characters, or goes for a nature walk. Playtime is the secret to a lasting love-filled life.

Western medicine doesn't have anything on playtime, so if you are feeling blue just take your mind to a fun place. Start to imagine new possibilities. Play is as much an emotional act as it is physical. It starts in the mind. The more imaginative you can be, the longer playtime can last, and the younger you will feel. I don't worry about getting older. The majority of my friends will stay 29 for the rest of their lives, scared of the big 30 even though that day has long passed for them, but I graciously accept every new day and every new year. Age is a beautiful thing when you love every second of your life.

The value of play dates back to the first humans ever to walk the earth. Cavemen who were primarily focused on surviving still made time to play, carving little cave people figures, playing games and interacting with their loved ones. Play becomes a useful survival tool; flipping through the National Geographic Channel we can see proof in baby animals learning their way through the world with play. Just look at the polar bear cubs wrestling around with their brothers and sisters. They push forward in life with a necessary dose of play. When I spend time around children, I am gently reminded that life is a big playground for them. Everything from rolling down the car window to walking between the cracks is a giant game. Therefore playtime becomes a basic need, a need that can only be met when we actively pursue it.

Playtime is something we need to think about. As adults we have conditioned ourselves to "schedule" time to play, we make an effort to carve out space in our lives for a vacation down the road, or a for a cushioned retirement package far off into the future. We work hard all week, and play on the weekends for a couple hours. Children don't schedule time to play, play is their lives. Everything is a giant wonderland waiting to be touched, smelled, and jumped on. So go out and play. Look at everything you do as an opportunity to appreciate its wonder and awe.

Adding more play into your life is as simple as looking at your current home environment. How can you make your home a fun home? Perhaps you need a refresher paint job or to add games into your environment. I am a big game person. I get very excited to play games so I have games sitting out. *The Big Book of Questions* is fun. When guests come over I plop open a page and ask funny questions, like, "Would you rather live on a tropical island or in the mountains?" Things like this get conversations going and involve the imagination. Enjoy making moments more fun by adding daily doses of play.

See the Light Side of Everything

There have been countless reports of people having near death experiences, and as they almost die they see "the light." Then they are jolted back to reality, wake up from their near death episode and the number one take away from that almost dead experience is not, "Holy crap I almost died." It's, "OMG, I need to lighten up and not take life so seriously. I better start living."

We don't all get second chances, but we can switch our path starting right now. If you feel unhappy, you have the power to choose happiness with your actions. It starts with your perception and how you treat the world. The way we see the world is a reflection of how we see ourselves. Remembering to treat ourselves kindly and laugh often is one way to appreciate life. In order to love our lives to the fullest, we can start by lightening up. When we learn to not take life so seriously, this is when we can truly be free.

I've been exercising this lately and I have seen a transformation in my world. New opportunities have come to me that otherwise wouldn't have because of my outlook on life. When I choose happy, kind, and loving thoughts, more happy, kind, and loving people and opportunities can come to me.

This can help in relationships, too. I remember a conversation I had with my ex—boyfriend. As I watched him get angry, I started to smile, and he quickly attacked, "Oh you think this is funny. This isn't funny to me." I laughed and said, "Well, yes, in the grand scheme of things, in the big picture this is funny. We are arguing about something so small when people are dying, and other people have disease and are suffering and losing family members. We have each other, we have our health, and we have the ability to laugh and smile, and I want to do it more. We have the ability to choose whether or not to argue, and I don't want to." At first he was shocked but then he started to laugh, too, and immediately we hugged and the argument was extinguished. "You don't have to attend every argument you are invited to" is a great quote from an anonymous writer.

Where are you grasping in your life? Are there any areas that you are taking too seriously, such as your job, your family, or yourself? Look at that and see how you can release resentment and control over the seriousness. On our mission to finding happy, we can let go of seriousness and let life flow more. Think about children and their outlook on the world. How often do you see a child super serious? They only learn to be poker faced through us inspiring adults. So let's learn a thing or two from the mini mes running around and adapt a happy-tude rather than an attitude.

Here are some simple ways to lighten up and let life flow:

1. Add more play to your life.
2. Play more games.
3. Look at the situation that is bothering you from a new perspective.
4. Laugh more.
5. Go outside and enjoy nature.
6. Turn your head up to the sun and let the light fall on to your face (this gives people an instant mental makeover).
7. Call a family member and tell them how you feel.
8. Pet a furry friend (refrain from wild furry friends unless you are comfortable with unpredictability).

9. Update your magic list.
10. Check off a magic list item.

Take things in stride and lighten up a little. After working through this guidebook we have released excuses, busted through fears and stepped into our happy self. Happy is always near and it's waiting for us to play with it.

In a Nutshell:

1. Trust your mini you because it will always guide you to happiness.
2. You can always reinvent yourself.
3. For a happy life, look at life as a giant recess.
4. Natural is beautiful.
5. The secret weapon for enjoying every moment of life is laughter and play.
6. Happy is always near and it's waiting for us to play with it.
7. When you embrace the *Play with the World* life, scheduling a vacation and planning things to look forward to are no longer necessary because your life is one big vacation.

Additional Resources:

Audio Meditation: *Find Your Happy: Motivational Mantras,* Track 14, "Lighten Up" (available on iTunes, amazon.com, and playwiththeworld. com shop).

CHAPTER EIGHTEEN

PLAY WITH THE WORLD

*"What lies behind us and what lies before us are tiny matters
compared to what lies within us." — Ralph Waldo Emerson*

We Are the Captains of Our Own Ships. Navigate Fiercely.

"A SHIP is supposed to carry you somewhere. If the FellowSHIP, FriendSHIP, OR RelationSHIP is not taking you to HIGHER LEVELS, then abandon that SHIP." This is an anonymous quote that many seminars and companies use for motivation. The notion expressed in this quote is one of the most basic principles of living a fulfilled life. Ask yourself how and where in life you are you growing as a person? Confidently go in that direction. If there are places you feel stuck, trapped or as if you are on a sinking ship it is time to release this and go on your merry way. We cannot be all that we are supposed to be when we have an anchor pulling us down.

The same way a ship is a reflection of our friendships it is also a mirror to our lives, and you, my dear friend, are the captain of your own ship. You now know that happiness is a choice and you can navigate to it any time you feel astray. Choosing loving thoughts and kind notions will always bring you back to happiness. You are accountable for your life and everything in your life is your creation. The people you meet, the places you go and the opportunities that come to you are in your life because of allow them or resist them. In the same way a ship calculates its position by the North Star at sea, you can navigate to your perfect life.

Life Is Your Creation

Navigate confidently in the direction you want to go and recognize that life is whatever you want to create. Pull out your giant crayons and paint and throw color, adventure and new opportunities onto that canvas. You create whatever you want. Believing and understanding this gives weight to the fact that if there is something in your life that you do not want, it is there with your permission. Everything in our lives is our creation, we have allowed this thing that we do not want to be in our reality because of our resistance to it.

Take, for example, a person who wants to lose weight. They are doing everything they can, including exercising and eating well. The weight can never come off if they think about what they don't want every time they don't exercise for their desired set time or stray from the diet, or resist what they see in the mirror. Always turn your thoughts to love, happiness and kindness for a fulfilling life. Once our friend releases the negative outlook about the weight, the weight WILL fall off. Create what you want. Pull out your magic list and tackle that bad boy because the reality is life is short and incredibly hard if we are doing, being, or experiencing anything we don't like. In any situation you always have three choices, to resist it (which causes more anxiety, stress, and frustration), accept it (which brings peace, love, and harmony), or move away from it. You choose, but don't continue to complain, moan, and gripe about anything that is no longer serving you, remove it completely. In doing this, you will open yourself up to new possibilities. New experiences can come to you and your creation is manifested. Remember to let it happen on its own time. Keep working towards your dream. Do not let go of your vision. Keep creating and sharing your dream. It will come true.

Relax, Release, and Surrender

When you feel yourself getting upset, whether things are not working the way you want them to, people are not acting the way you want or giving you what you need, or your dream is not coming true fast enough, the first thing to do is stop and relax. Literally chill yourself out by taking a few breaths. Breathe in light, breathe "garbage, negative thoughts, fears bad stuff," out. Breathe in light, breathe out. Do this mantra and repeat this a few times until you feel better. Then release this energy. Let go of expectations, outcomes, and worry. Just let go and surrender to the experience. Surrender to the outcome that is your current reality. Let it go without worrying about the outcome. Whatever is will be, whatever it is. It is what it is. Surrendering to the current reality is a gentle reminder to yourself that everything is in its right order.

Me-Mandatories

We have done a lot of work. This guide has helped you clear out a lot of space so you can create the life you really want, love and cherish. It is important to continue to practice. I found one of the best ways to do this is by creating a Me-Mandatory list. This is basically your must haves for living each day true to yourself. You know what makes you feel good, what makes your spirit sing, and your body-rocking glow, so put these things into a list and hold them close to you. I type mine on the notes of my phone and pull it up for a refreshing reminder. This list is kind of like New Year's resolutions only rather than resolving to follow them, you abide by them. Why set such stringent rules for yourself? It's because you will feel, look and be better. This list is not a strict list; it is an inspirational list for your true self to have a guidance system. Let's create a list.

Awesome Opportunity:

1. Ask yourself when you feel best in your life, what are you doing? Who are you with? Where are you?
2. Ask yourself what you value most in life. (See Chapter 7 for guidance.)
3. Create a list around this attribute.

For example, my list goes something like this:
1. I move my body and sweat once a day for at least 40 minutes.
2. I balance myself with a daily practice of yoga and meditation.
3. I spend time in nature every day for at least ten minutes.
4. I write and/or read every day.
5. I only eat foods and drink beverages that support my higher well being and allow me to stay connected to my source.
6. I appreciate the moment and live in the present.
7. I dream big, and then dream even bigger.
8. I am fully available and present to my life. I love every moment to its fullest.
9. The world is my office and I play with it daily.
10. My mission: I share my experiences and message with the masses and inspire people to make the most out of their lives.

I call this mandatory-me list the, "Super Me Mantras." Making a Super Me Mantra list will help you feel more connected to your life and true self. I stray from mine from time to time, and that is okay. I recognize that no one is perfect and it is not about perfection. It is about doing the best that you can at any given moment. When you get off track, rather than beating yourself up mentally, tell yourself it's okay. Remind yourself that you are doing the best you can, then focus on the good things you did do. Falling off or getting off track, does not mean it is over. It takes time to master the Mandatory-Me list, but when you live it, you are more free and fulfilled.

Those Who Are Confident in the Outcome Can Afford to Wait

After all of the work we have done, you have created a place for play, abundance, and fulfillment to coexist. When you apply the steps shared in this book, you will be living in happiness. Remember thought that happiness is not an ever constant. We must always choose happy and that choice is a conscious one. When we have dreams, we get clear about them and then work towards them we must remember to let go of the outcome.

A Course in Miracles teaches that those who are certain of the outcome can afford to wait and wait without worry, which means that you trust that whatever the outcome is will be in your favor. Often people will hold on to the dream so tightly that there is no breathing room for it to grow or even manifest. The emphasis should be on holding the vision of that dream. Do visualization meditations. You can download my *Find Your Happy Motivational Mantras* CD on *playwiththeworld.com* for extra guidance. Focus on what you want, not on how or when it will come to you. This is the key element in keeping your happy: picture, feel, and focus on what you want. I am living proof that this works and is a valid way to keep your happiness.

As you know I declared my dream to be a travel writer while I was working at a advertising job in Chicago, and the idea of traveling the world and sharing my experiences with people seemed so far removed. Yet I thought about it every day. I started to meet people who were in the publishing industry and really successful travel writers. I was soon given opportunities to write for local magazines and newspapers about local events and places to travel to. Within a few months, I was published in many inspirational blogs and other books. All of this was happening while I was still trying to force an advertising desk job into my life.

I changed companies and cities searching for my happy, while my hobby, writing, was my one true love. It was my sustenance that kept me alive. Find your sustenance, that one thing you couldn't do without, that one thing that you love to do more than anything, that you would do for free because you love it so much. The best authors I know are mission driven, they have a purpose, a mission, to deliver their message and they believe in it so much that they would do it for little or no money. The thing about mission-focused people is the money will always follow. When you do something you love, when you live your purpose, you will make mounds of money. The most successful people in the world are living their purpose, and they are millionaires for following their hearts.

My purpose is writing sharing this message in coaching, workshops and lectures as well as travel writing is what I was born to do. When I do it, I feel connected to the world, and myself and I am inspired at every turn. Find your purpose, and you will *Find Your Happy*. Releasing the how and when will determine your success. The past few years I was not concerned with it happening overnight or how it was going to happen. Certain things needed to come into play before I could just go around the world and write about it. I had to grow as a person. I needed to meet specific people in order to help me get to where I was supposed to be. Always trust the process. When you are not sure why your goal is taking a long time, be patient. It will happen when it is supposed to. Your only job is to keep believing in and KNOWING that it is on its way.

Life Is a Journey, Not a Destination

Letting go of the outcome is your final step. Once you do that you can appreciate the journey rather than the destination. The destination is part of the journey, because once we reach each destination a new one appears on the horizon. Loving the moment and being present in it will help the journey be more enjoyable. When you embrace the *Play with the World* mentality your happiness can flow. You are no longer consumed with worry, fear, or anxiety. Get ready to step into the new you because opportunities will always come to you. Enjoy the ride.

Love Your Life to the Fullest

If there is one thing to remember as you embark into the new territory of awesome, happy you, it is to remember to smile. Life is fun, and the world is supposed to be your playground. So choose to love your life at every moment. You chose happiness. I congratulate you for doing the hard-core work necessary to dig through the grime and get to happy. You, my friend, are awesome, and your happy will forever shine through. I want to leave you with the wisdom of Aristotle, "Happiness depends upon ourselves." We will always have a choice in life. At every given moment of your life, you can choose happy over fear. You can choose love over hate. Make a conscious choice to be happy and you can and will change the world.

In a Nutshell:

1. Your life is your ship, navigate it.
2. Always turn your thoughts to love, happiness, and kindness for a fulfilling life.
3. When you are connected to your true self you are in pure joy and doing what you love.
4. Let go of when and how, and your dream will be realized.
5. Enjoy the journey; there is no destination.

Additional Resources:

Audio Meditation: *Find Your Happy: Motivational Mantras,* Track 15, "Follow Your Heart" (available on iTunes, amazon.com, and playwiththeworld.com shop).

Epilogue

Here I sit finishing my book in one of the most beautiful places in the world. I made a declaration and promise to myself, when I left corporate. "The world is my office and I play with it daily." At the time I was stuck behind a desk in a giant warehouse doing design work for corporations who cared more about expanding their wallets then helping others. Now just a short time later I am "stuck" in Saint Lucia, on a travel writing assignment, all of the other journalists have flown home. I am looking out at the Caribbean Sea and recognizing the true potency of everything shared in this book. I live my happy every moment and I am living my dream. My trip to Saint Lucia was supposed to end yesterday, but because of flight cancellations to JFK because of the weather, I am here for another week. It's an all-expense paid trip to paradise, courtesy of my angels. How is that for finding your happy? I am beaming with joy and gratitude because loving your life and living your purpose is what it's all about. When you do, you will get gifts from the universe and the angels will say thank you for being you and give you magical miracles, like a free trip to Saint Lucia.

All of this happened because I let go of the when and how. I knew that my dream would become real. I felt it and believed in it with every fiber of my body. You must believe in yourself and your dreams because they will come true. Once you step into your purpose and your real happy, you will be a shining light of golden opportunity. Life will flow and you will certainly glow.

Acknowledgments

I want to first and foremost thank you for reading this book. I hope you have found more peace, excitement, and joy in your own life story. I want to thank every person I have ever met, and all of you who continue to support me in sharing this message through my life's work.

I want to thank my friends and family, you helped shape, guide and teach me more about life, relationships and myself. I'm humbly grateful for the time we have together. To all my teachers, I love you with all my heart.

Life is a creative adventure and mine is more complete with all of you in it. Now let's all go play with the world.

THE JOURNEY IS
THE REWARD.
-CHINESE PROVERB

playwiththeworld.com

References and Resources

Arylo, Christine. *Choosing ME Before WE: Every Woman's Guide to Life and Love.* Novato, CA: New World Library, 2009.

Bacon, Summer. *This School Called Planet Earth.* Flagstaff, AZ: Light Technology Publishing, 2005.

Bernstein, Gabrielle. *Spirit Junkie: A Radical Road to Self-Love and Miracles.* New York: Harmony Books, 2011.

Bernstein, Gabrielle. *Add More Ing to Your Life: A Hip Guide to Happiness.* Random House Inc, 2011.

Brittan, Rhonda. *Fearless Loving: Eight Simple Truths That Will Change the Way You Date, Mate, and Relate.* New York: Dutton, 2003.

Byrne, Rhonda. *The Secret.* New York: Atria Books. Hillsboro, OR: Beyond Words Pub., 2006.

Canfield, Jack, Ed. *Chicken Soup for the Soul.* Cos Cob, CT: Chicken Soup for the Soul Publishing.

Carlson, Kristine. *Don't Sweat the Small Stuff for Women: Simple and Practical Ways to Do What Matters Most and Find Time for You.* Publisher: New York: Hyperion, 2001.

Carlson, Richard. *Don't Sweat the Small Stuff — and It's All Small Stuff: Simple Ways to Keep the Little Things from Taking over Your Life.* New York: Hyperion, 1997.

Carr, Kris. *Crazy Sexy Diet: Eat Your Veggies, Ignite Your Spark, and Live Like You Mean It!* Guilford, CT: Skirt, 2011.

Deschene, Lori. "40 Ways to Let Go and Feel Less Pain." Tinybuddha.

Dwyer, Wayne W. *The Power of Intention: Learning to Co-Create Your World Your Way.* Carlsbad, CA: Hay House, 2004.

Ferriss, Timothy. *The 4-Hour Workweek: Escape 9-5, Live Anywhere, and Join the New Rich.* New York: Crown Publishers, 2007.

Foundation for Inner Peace. *A Course in Miracles.* Mill Valley, CA: Foundation for Inner Peace, 3rd ed., 2007.

Griggs Lawrence, Robyn. *The Wabi-Sabi House: The Japanese Art of Imperfect Beauty.* New York: Clarkson Potter, 2004.

Hay, Louise. *You Can Heal Your Life.* Carlsbad, CA: Hay House, 2004.

Hicks, Esther. *Money and the Law of Attraction.* Carlsbad, CA: Hay House, Inc., 2008.

Hicks, Jerry and Esther. *Ask and It Is Given: Learning to Manifest Your Desires.* Carlsbad, CA: Hay House, 2004.

Kashdan, Todd B. Kashdan. "Why Are We Afraid of Having Regrets? Learn 5 Scientific Discoveries About Regret." *Psychology Today*, Aug 19, 2010.

Kasl, Charlotte Davis. *If the Buddha Dated: A Handbook for Finding Love on a Spiritual Path.* New York: Penguin/Arkana, 1999.

Sills, Judith. *The Comfort Trap Or, What If You're Riding a Dead Horse?* New York: Viking, 2004.

Silverstone, Alicia. *The Kind Diet: A Simple Guide to Feeling Great, Losing Weight, and Saving the Planet.* Emmaus, PA: Rodale, 2009.

Yes Man. Dir. Peyton Reed. Perfs. Jim Carrey, Zooey Deschanel, Bradley Cooper. Warner Bros. Entertainment Inc., 2008.

Websites

www.playwiththeworld.com

www.kristinecarlson.com

www.crazysexylife.com

www.herfuture.com

www.mindbodygreen.com

www.thedailylove.com

www.tinybuddha.com

Final Note

Thank you for choosing to Find Your Happy.

As a special thank you, email your book purchase receipt to info@ playwiththeworld.com to redeem loads of free gifts from affiliate best-selling authors and happiness experts.

For more information about Shannon Kaiser and her signature Play with the World approach to life and breakthrough transformational workshops, lectures and events please visit:

www.Playwiththeworld.com

About the Author

Shannon Kaiser is an Advertising award winning senior art director, who left her successful career to follow her heart and be a writer.

Today she is a travel writer, inspirational author, motivational speaker and creator of Playwiththeworld.com. A site dedicated to helping others fall in love with their life through, articles, videos, books, podcast, lectures and more.

She knows happiness and wellness and shares her knowledge authentically and from her own "been there and learned the tough way" perspective. An adventure girl at heart, her advice is shared with an uplifting, playful and motivational manner.

She is the travel tip editor for *Healing Lifestyles and Spas*, and a Destination Travel Editor for *Examiner.com*. A handful of her motivational stories have been published in *Chicken Soup for The Soul* and her opinions have been shared on ABC AM Northwest KATU Morning Show.

Shannon also works with a variety of individuals and businesses – serving as their Design Guru, website designer, advertising agency, Brand Development, and writer.

For speaking, and press inquires contact
info@playwiththeworld.com

For coaching sessions and inquires contact
coach@playwiththeworld.com

Website: www.playwiththeworld.com

Notes

Notes

Notes

Notes

Notes

Notes

Notes

CPSIA information can be obtained at www.ICGtesting.com
Printed in the USA
LVOW12s1113130314

377273LV00001B/61/P